The authors of this book are neither naïve or irresponsible. They are aware that Russian conquest might well follow the West's renunciation of nuclear arms; they are aware, too, that life under the Soviet masters would be unspeakably harsh, and that not only Christian, but even human values, would be imperilled. Yet to defend these values by nuclear war, they argue, is to betray the very values we seek to defend.

WALTER STEIN. Lecturer in Philosophy and English Literature, Extra-Mural Department, University of Leeds. In the late 'forties, as a student, he was one of the founder-editors of *Humanitas,* a national staff-student review, already much concerned with the morality of atomic weapons. He has contributed to critical and religious journals, and is now writing a book on tragedy.

G. E. M. ANSCOMBE. Lecturer in Philosophy at Somerville College, Oxford. Her work includes the translation of Wittgenstein's *Philosophical Investigations* and other of Wittgenstein's posthumous works. She is also well known for her important study *Intention,* for her authoritative *Introduction to Wittgenstein's Tractatus,* and is preparing a study of St. Augustine for the *Cambridge History of Ancient and Medieval Philosophy.*

R. A. MARKUS. Lecturer in Medieval History, University of Liverpool. Another founder-editor of *Humanitas.* His academic interests include the history of philosophy, and he is an authority in patristic studies. He is joint author (with A. H. Armstrong) of *Christian Faith and Greek Philosophy* and is preparing a study of St. Augustine for the *Cambridge History of Ancient and Medieval Philosophy.*

P. T. GEACH. Reader in Logic, University of Birmingham. Has made distinguished contributions to logic, metaphysics and epistemology. He has edited and translated Descartes and Frege, and his volume on *Mental Acts,* which is especially concerned with the nature and formation of concepts, has profoundly influenced contemporary discussion.

ROGER SMITH. Lecturer at the Liverpool College of Art. He has made a particular study of the work and teaching of Eric Gill. A Pax Council member from 1951-4 and a contributor of various reviews.

NUCLEAR WEAPONS

— A CATHOLIC RESPONSE —

G. E. M. Anscombe
R. A. Markus
P. T. Geach
Roger Smith
Walter Stein

Foreword by Mgr. T. D. Roberts, S. J.
ARCHBISHOP OF SYGDEA

SHEED AND WARD
NEW YORK

CONTENTS

Should the evil consequences of adopting this method of warfare ever become so extensive as to pass utterly beyond the control of man, then indeed its use must be rejected as immoral. In that event, it would no longer be a question of "defence" against injustice and necessary "protection" of legitimate possessions, but of the annihilation, pure and simple, of all human life within the affected area. That is not lawful on any title.

Pope Pius XII, *Address to the World Medical Association, September 1954*

We are not going to reduce our nuclear capability. Personally, I have never believed in nuclear limited war. I do not know how you could build a limit into it when you use any kind of nuclear bang.

Mr. Roswell Gilpatric, *Deputy Defence Secretary, U.S.A., June 1961*

THIS BOOK is a Roman Catholic contribution to the subject of Western defence. As such, it addresses itself in the first place to Catholics, in the hope of establishing a valid application of principles to the immensely urgent problems of the nuclear age. It is, however, equally concerned to engage in discussion with other Christians, as well as with those who would not claim this title: we are all Westerners confronted by a common challenge, and there is nothing to prevent our conversing together with profit.

The book is intended as a unified examination of the moral and spiritual issues involved, and there has been much discussion among ourselves to achieve a maximum of coherence in our statement. The first chapter outlines our approach. Miss Anscombe then examines the moral distinction between killing and murder in war, and applies this analysis to the problem of nuclear war. Dr. Markus draws out the implications of this analysis for the policy of deterrence. Mr. P. T. Geach meets some final lines of objection to our case. Mr. Roger Smith reviews traditional formulations of the "just war" concept and the Catholic Church's present witness in these matters. And my concluding chapter seeks to relate our case to the debate on nuclear weapons in general and to the underlying spiritual currents of our time.

We should like to express our gratitude to Archbishop Roberts, for his Foreword, and to our friends and sympathizers who have given us many kinds of important assistance.   W.S.

FOREWORD

ANY CONTRIBUTORS to a volume like this are more likely to be rewarded with bricks than bouquets; for they suggest the need for new applications of old truths—and applications of a very challenging kind. Yet may these writers take courage from the success of pioneers, as in England where Sir Stephen King-Hall's long struggle for common sense applied to strategy is beginning to bear fruit; Christians in some other countries are ploughing a less lonely furrow, as I realized when an invitation came from Vienna to give a retreat in Spain (of all places!) to an international group of Catholics in close touch with Rome. The purpose of such retreats is to study the Christian tradition of peace, in an atmosphere of prayer.

But time presses. There is no mistaking the note of confidence characteristic of the new Soviet diplomacy. Earlier disciples of Lenin and Stalin had to lie, to misrepresent Christianity in order to produce the conviction in whole nations that "religion is the opium of the people". But their lies were far less damaging to Christianity than the actual connection between the Russian Church and abuses of the Czarist régime. So of France, both before and since its Revolution. So of much of South America. It was not a communist who said that the workers of the nineteenth century had been lost to Christianity but Pope Pius XI.

Every Christian generation adds its own sad meaning to our Lord's words deploring the folly of his own children in contrast to the conduct of their opponents. If we put in the place of the workers lost to Christ, by the indifference of

Christians, today's millions of half-Christians in Europe drifting into doubt and despair, we see one reason why Soviet rulers are so cheerful.

It pleases them that the Western world has been lured into attempts to defend values fundamentally Christian by means at least questionable from a Christian point of view, so that it is increasingly divided in spirit.

The conditioned communist has no problem here at all: whether to wipe out a hundred million people with H-bombs is no more of a *moral* problem than the liquidation of millions in the Ukraine or in China. One question alone is relevant: "will this help to establish world communism?" The West is by comparison weighed down with cumbersome armour. "Shall we use these means to repel communism?" is open to a hundred different answers from a hundred free people, not only because they are free, but because the Western tradition suggests at least the possibility of a God to whom we are responsible and whose Image is one who never stooped to the methods of His enemies.

Yet we *must* resist evil. How, then, if violence should have so far overreached itself that war must destroy the very persons and values to be defended? Resistance by non-violent means? Until not long ago, even to put the question might have seemed madness. Today a Catholic theologian dares to write a book on *Non-Violence and the Christian Conscience*. Père Régamey, O.P., searches in vain for Catholic material for his subject. He finds it chiefly in the Hindu Ghandi. "Was it the Mahatma's very devotion to the person of Christ that made him exaggerate the iniquities and follies of organized Christianity?" Ghandi's use of a power in the moral order comparable to atomic energy in the physical may perhaps point a way where all other ways seem closed.

Inevitably, the application of moral measures to a threat

without precedent gives rise to differences like those among scientists experimenting with nuclear energy. But in this world-wide *moral* experiment there will be no second or third chance to fall back on! Among Catholics, clear, authoritative guidance is being sought just by those who have toiled hardest to reach a decision. Thus, the writers of this book, carefully examining these questions in the light of reason and tradition, are agreed in affirming some very decisive conclusions. They are far from regarding the absence of explicit official prohibitions, in this field of contemporary defence, as grounds for suspending the operations of conscience. And they do not ask for the Church's guidance to indulge a passion for new infallible declarations. They feel, however, that it would hardly be fair to blame anyone for approaching these matters purely in terms of expediency, so long as scientists, soldiers and politicians are vocal, religious leaders silent or ambiguous —if not in intent, at any rate in effect. They are conscious of a supremely urgent need for an effective Christian witness in this matter. And they fear that respect for Christian authority is suffering by neglect of this need. If, on the other hand, the Church responds to this challenge in full accord with her mission, what could more fittingly proclaim to this desperately bewildered age what manner of Rock she is?

What, then, could be more timely or crucial than the consideration of these questions by the Second Vatican Council, or perhaps, as I have previously suggested, by a "Council for Survival", more loosely associated with the Vatican Council proper? Rome, Canterbury, Istanbul and all other Christian bodies are interested, as are non-Christians, in survival and salvation. Their combined action in this matter would immensely strengthen the forces of religion, and might help to unity in God's own time. Catholics may have much to learn from Quakers, for example; the West may have much to learn from Eastern thought. All have certainly much to learn from scientists and strategic thinkers about the facts of contemporary "defence". And if co-operation between German scientists with Russians, and of Germans with Americans, has contributed so much to the nuclear threat, surely the united resources of morality, religion and common sense can combine to face the resulting crisis, urgently decide whatever must now be decided, and at least study seriously the trail blazed by pioneers of non-violent resistance to evil, towards a defence that could defend. ✠ T. D. ROBERTS, S.J.

Archbishop of Sygdea

I

INTRODUCTORY:
THE DEFENCE OF THE WEST

Walter Stein

> "If we believe we should defend our civiliz-
> ation and our way of life, then we should
> be prepared to defend it at whatever the
> cost."
>
> *Mr. Harold MacMillan*

EVERYBODY DETESTS the H-bomb. Few are prepared to do
without it. No H-bomb, no Western freedom, remains the
dominant verdict. And this may well be right. Our military
security rests on nuclear defence.

Indeed, it seems improbable that it will ever be safe for the
West to relinquish these weapons. Even if, through mutual
fear, a serious agreement for disarmament and control were
achieved, we should not have achieved security. Britain alone
has long possessed enough nuclear explosive to destroy every
large city in the world; the United States and Soviet stock-
piles are vastly larger. Does anyone imagine that a fool-proof
system of inspection could be worked out which would
guarantee that none of this stock has been hidden away?
Much could be done (especially by controlling the means of
delivery) to diminish the consequent risks, but vast risks
would remain to be lived with. Leaving the H-bomb aside,
it would not need many Hiroshima-type bombs, wielded by
one side alone, to determine the outcome of any conflict. Can
the West, then, afford to trust Moscow's word in this matter?
Or Moscow to trust the West's? And—in the long run, even
more challenging—how, if we were stripped of these weapons,
how, in the last resort, could we balance the increasingly
explosive pressure of Chinese numbers?

It is in a general East-West *rapprochement*—the radical

treatment of international infections, together with general disarmament arrangements—that our hopes have come to centre. Men must have hope; and, no doubt, the gathering urge towards international co-operation in these days, in spite of the bitterest setbacks, reasserts our humanity across immensities of terror and estrangement. Yet, where it would reach for *security*, this urge may itself be blinkered. We may indeed hope that the necessary gestures of trust might not be abused. We may hope that ideological conflict can indefinitely be contained within "peaceful competition"; that the politics of power that have mainly prevailed in history will finally yield to politics of mental strife. And we may hope that a whole-hearted system of disarmament and inspection might so reduce the risks of betrayal that, even if someone attempted to break loose, the system would suffice to bring him to terms. The fact remains that anything short of a World State would leave us so far from "secure" that it might actually seem more hazardous to risk betrayal after disarming than to risk betrayal whilst one remains armed.

It does not follow that we should not continue to seek agreed disarmament, only that we should be serious in striving to bring this about—and that we should be serious in facing the risks. We may then find that there is in fact only one realistic basis for such a policy (however rarely this may be confessed or perceived): a readiness, if need be, to disarm unilaterally, or, in the last resort, to fall back on non-violent resistance, *as if* we had thus unilaterally disarmed.

For it is not necessary to postulate tortuous Machiavellian traps to be left with a lingering insecurity, even if "controlled disarmament" could be achieved. The tortuousness is inherent in the situation. Whatever the measures of disarmament agreed, whatever the stages and means of control, there can

18

be no assurance of ultimate safety. Apart from all other considerations, we have to reckon with the immense and ineradicable anxieties on each side that the other might, after all, be concealing a fraction of its stocks. Each side not only knows that the other *could* conceal nuclear stocks, but knows that the other side is aware of a converse danger—and so all the more likely to be *in fact* driven to concealment; simply, therefore, in sheer self-protection, just in case this should be the case. . . . And, once stocks were thus to be preserved, there is no telling what might occur in the extremity of a subsequent crisis.

Discussions of disarmament, in the past decade, have been so hypnotically centred on nuclear weapons that there has been very little public attention to the equally serious—and even more intractable—problems of biological and chemical warfare. The appalling efficiency of biological and chemical weapons, perfected by post-war research, and the virtual impossibility of controlling their production, may well render them the most obstinate problem of all. Everything that can be urged against the chances of real security in the atomic field must apply with even greater force to these easily dispersed agents, which could be produced, in huge quantities, at very short notice.[1]

If—and only if—our basic line of defence is non-violent resistance, these uncertainties can be lived with with open eyes—and perhaps turned to creative account. In any case, apart perhaps from very clearly restricted "police" actions, there is now no valid alternative, morally, to such a commit-

[1] cf. the symposium in the *Bulletin of Atomic Scientists*, Summer 1960, which draws attention to this virtual impossibility of control, and hence calls for the creation of an international conscience among scientists and for international *pledges* to terminate preparations for the use of such agents in war.

ment. The establishment of these assertions is the purpose of this book.

1. THE ARGUMENT FROM EXPEDIENCY

A strong case can be made for a basic commitment to non-violent defence in present circumstances on strategic and political grounds. This case is becoming increasingly familiar.

Like the demands for unilateral nuclear disarmament, to which it is related, this case has a special relevance to Britain and Western Europe; though some of these arguments are no less relevant to the position of the United States. (The main difference is, of course, that whilst Europe recognizes its own extreme vulnerability and, at the same time, the immense strategic and political reserves of America across the Atlantic, America cannot but be conscious of its essential self-dependence.)

The case has a positive and a negative aspect. Negatively, it rests on the three facts that no amount of nuclear power can guarantee Western security; that no military means at all can shield us against communism as an ideological force; and that the concept of nuclear war has indeed obliterated the concept of military defence. (A great deal of the argument, both here and in subsequent chapters, though stated in terms of nuclear strategy, equally applies to biological and chemical weapons.)

That nuclear power cannot guarantee Western security is evident both in theory and from experience. It did not, for instance, prevent Soviet infiltration into the Middle East, nor —in spite of Western reactions—the supression of the Hungarian revolt. The very enormity of strategic nuclear weapons disqualifies them as instruments of limited defence. What they do provide is an over-all "balance of terror" that discourages naked large-scale aggression, plus a tremendous general stiffening of the risks attending local coups. Now, apart from the fact that strategic nuclear power cannot provide effective local protection, there are at least three sorts of situation in which a nuclear war might be unleashed (and whatever emerges from such a war will not be the security of our civilization). (i) A local conflict—in Africa, for instance, or in a satellite country —might, in spite of the great stiffening of risks already mentioned, set off a chain-reaction towards total war. (ii) In the atmosphere of fear and strain generated by a prolonged nuclear stalemate, one side or the other may eventually suffer a failure of nerve. A rumour of enemy war preparations or a mistake relating to radar signals, might thus easily precipitate a plunge into actual war. (iii) And it is not necessary to rehearse the fantastic hazards that would result from the imminent diffusion of more and more nuclear weapons among more and more governments throughout the world. We may take it as established that the "security" provided by nuclear weapons is far from complete—and is achieved at the price of the most radical insecurities men have ever been exposed to.

It is, moreover, self-evident that no military means at all can shield us against communism as an ideological force. Ideologically, communism is an infection that can only be arrested by better health. Military strength is as irrelevant from this point of view as it is to the destruction of cancer. Even a defeat of Russia and China might actually be followed by a resurgence of communism throughout the world. The enormous sums spent on nuclear armaments might be used more effectively to combat communism by a world-wide campaign against poverty and the evils that make the communist solution attractive.

But not only is nuclear defence unable to guarantee security; not only are military means incapable of stemming communism as an idea: "nuclear defence" is simply a contradiction in terms. This has been shown again and again in recent discussions—and indeed is presupposed in official N.A.T.O. thinking. The policy of "deterrence" recognizes that our best hope, in a full-scale nuclear war, (short of actually starting it) is to inflict similar feats of annihilation upon our enemy as our enemy has just inflicted upon ourselves. Worries about the "missile gap", vulnerability of bases, "credibility" and so on, are all primarily worries about the capacity of "the deterrent" to *deter*: few of our leaders are apparently troubled by the question whether the hope of annihilating even though one has already been annihilated can amount to a rational concept of defence.

It is clear that the security provided by nuclear weapons has its limits. In the light of this consideration—and its corollary, that without nuclear weapons military security is now altogether unthinkable—the alternative of non-violent resistance acquires an unprecedented practical attraction. What we used to dismiss as the panacea of political enthusiasts, now imposes itself as a strategy for the tough-minded. At the least, it can no longer be precluded from serious thought.

Yet it must be admitted that the force of these arguments is negative. They show that military security is now absurd. It is only when this fact has been grasped—really assimilated into our image of the world—that we are likely to cease chasing after such "security". But even when we have thus broken through what Sir Stephen King-Hall calls "the thought-barrier in defence thinking", there remain enormous intractable problems when it comes to a positive advocacy of non-violent defence. There is quite a lot of available information about historical uses of non-violence. There is the outstanding achievement of Ghandi. And Sir Stephen himself outlines some interesting plans for non-violent action in our situation, towards the end of his *Defence in the Nuclear Age*. Yet does any of this really measure up to the problems of a life-and-death struggle of the kind we are concerned with, a world-wide struggle for ideological survival—with the men who "saved Hungary from the fascists"—and whose ritual clamour for peace is punctuated by oubursts of savage diplomatic aggression and threats of nuclear punishment? Or with the men who "liberated Tibet"—and who openly continue to believe in the efficacy, if not the inevitability, of international violence?

This, too, must be faced: the positive case for non-violent resistance, in our situation, appears to be as implausible in terms of prudence, as the negative arguments seem compelling. We shall return to this problem in the last chapter.

2. THE MORAL ARGUMENT

Nuclear defence cannot provide security; and in this sense we do not surrender our security if we renounce it. Yet there are important senses in which we should nevertheless be less "secure" without nuclear weapons, especially in view of what has just been admitted about non-violent resistance. Secure or insecure, however, there is now no *moral* alternative to an unconditional renunciation of "the deterrent": this is the central submission of this book.

In essence, the plea is very simple indeed: (i) that some things are intolerable, irrespective of circumstances; that total war is thus absolutely intolerable; and that "nuclear defence" means total war; (ii) that the mere willingness to *risk* a war that could annihilate civilization, poison the whole of this planet, and for ever violate the life of the future, if life survives, is a wickedness without parallel, a blasphemy against Creation; and (iii) that the policy of "deterrence" involves a conditional willingness to unleash such a war—and is therefore not only wicked in what it risks, but in terms of implicit *intention*.

A decade and a half after Hiroshima and Nagasaki, and nearly a decade after the testing of a bomb whose destructive power is fifteen times greater than the total weight of bombs dropped on Germany during the last war, this plea is still struggling to gain so much as a serious hearing. There is now a thought-race, over against the arms-race, to master the new facts of death. But the perception that things like these *simply must not be*—the simple acknowledgement of our status as human beings—remains strangely muddled and muffled. Even those whose thought and attitudes clearly spring from this kind of perception, often prefer to clothe themselves in elaborate pragmatic expertise (as if to acknowledge such claims as decisive must be a little embarrassing in its naïvety). And elsewhere, there are vast and complicated ranges of resistance to this plea—if only the resistance of silence. It thus becomes necessary to restate this essentially simple plea in precise, analytic detail, in the hope of driving out mistaken analyses. (One cannot, of course, hope to drive out a determination to by-pass or irrationally overwhelm it.)

Certainly, there are strong logical and psychological difficulties that may obstruct clear vision. One reason, for instance, why this case has made so little headway is that the notion of total war is one to which we have been steadily acclimatized. There is, it seems, a long unbroken ascent of military developments towards Hiroshima, with no footholds for moral distinctions. Before Hiroshima, there was saturation bombing; and before that, more haphazard raids on civilians. In the background of these is the combined raiding of military and civilian targets—and, for that matter, heavy artillery shellings. The whole concept of conscript armies already implies a large measure of "totality". From there, you can go further and further back, pausing at the atrocities of the Thirty Years' War or the sacking of medieval towns. Finally, you may be denying any essential difference between an H-bomb attack and a battle with swords and shields.

Now it is no doubt difficult to insert a line into this sort of progression; and there may be much discussion about where precisely it should be drawn. What is certain is that a line must be drawn somewhere, and that nuclear warfare stands far to the wrong side of it.

There is nothing odd about this combination of open-mindedness and certainty. There may be much discussion about whether Strasbourg is really a French or German town, and I may be unwilling to commit myself; but this does not mean I have any doubt about whether Paris is French or German. It is common, indeed usual, to be uncertain of a boundary but quite certain of what lies well to the east or west of it. This is especially the case when we are dealing with something that shades off from one extreme to another. We all know when a man is clean-shaven, and we know what it is for a man to be bearded. But what is it that makes a man bearded? Is it having one hair? or two? or three? or thirty? We can imagine a man saying that if it is impossible to settle for some definite number, if there is no such thing as the exact number of hairs which make a man bearded, then there is no such thing as the difference between having a beard and not having one. Of course, this is a simple and notorious logical fallacy. But while nobody is likely to commit this in cases such as this text-book example's, we may easily slip into fallacies of this kind where we are dealing with matters involving us more deeply. Thus the fallacy is especially prevalent in discussions of defence ethics. The existence of an unbroken chain of "degrees" between the primitive warrior's club and the modern man's H-bomb should not, however, obscure the difference between them.

Here the line has to be drawn between killing enemy combatants in a just war, which may be legitimate, and the deliberate killing of non-combatants (or "harmless"), which is murder.

We recognize that some such line can be drawn, and we show that we recognize it, by the fact that (unless we are pacifists or cynics) we think it is one thing to be a soldier and another to be a murderer. We do not seriously think of soldiers as "licensed murderers" or of murderers as un-licensed soldiers. We think that it is possible, or at least that it used to be possible, for a soldier to do his job without moral guilt.

As Miss G. E. M. Anscombe will show, in her chapter, "War and Murder", the primary job of a soldier is to defend the community against a particular form of attack—direct physical violence. In order to fulfil this important and honour-able purpose he may use certain extreme measures; for ex-ample, he may, of course, kill enemy troops if this is the only practicable way of protecting the community against them. It is important to see that the right to kill is not something that belongs to a soldier because he has a uniform but because he has a certain job to do. Troops may be used for many other purposes—quelling riots, or policing a conquered country, for example: in these circumstances they do not have the same right to use extreme measures. Similarly, the man who may be killed is not just any man who wears enemy uniform but a man who cannot otherwise be prevented from carrying out his present activity of violence; thus to shoot prisoners of war who are not engaged in hostilities is just ordinary murder. If we may not kill a man simply because he wears enemy uniform, still less may we kill him simply because he belongs to the enemy country or subscribes to the enemy's religion or political ideology. On the other hand, if a man is directly engaged in hostilities against the community, we may prevent him by killing, whether or not he is wearing a uniform. Any such man, in or out of uniform, is for the time being a combatant; he ceases to be a combatant as soon as he presents no immediate danger of physical violence.

Now, of course, the line between combatants and non-combatants is one of those which it is difficult to fix exactly, particularly is it difficult to draw it in the heat of action; yet, nevertheless, there are large areas which unquestionably lie on either side of the line. If it is right to kill enemy troops, what about civilians supplying their weapons? If it is right to kill munitions-workers, what about those supplying the forces with food? What, moreover, of all those who—in coal-mines or steel-works or laboratories—stand behind the immediate war-suppliers? And of those who, simply by performing the most unaggressive jobs, right down to hospital-nursing and hair-cutting, keep the economy in being and thereby assist the war-effort? Is "totality" not implicit in modern societies?

At this point it is only necessary to repeat that difficulties about the drawing of lines do not dispense from conscientiousness; to suggest that, when all has been said, there remains a qualitative abyss between a pilot's or munitions-worker's job and a barber's; and that a high proportion of any population consists of children, full-time mothers, pensioners and sick people. Of course, if someone is so inclined, he can reply that mothers rear children and are good for their husbands, that children will one day be workers or even soldiers—and are, in fact, already knitting socks for the troops—that pensioners can do all sorts of things in a crisis, and that sick people frequently get well again. Moralizing can have its moments.

Here we should perhaps pause to observe that the legitimate killing of combatants is something horrible. War would be full of horrors even without the murder of non-combatants.

27

It is important to say this because many people suppose that the objection to killing non-combatants is simply that the horrors of war ought to be kept within some conventional bounds. But the objection to murdering non-combatants is not simply that it makes war a degree more horrible, but that it is wicked. The killing of combatants is indeed a necessary evil—something ghastly which we may find ourselves bound to do; the killing of non-combatants is a *moral* evil, something which we have never the right to do.

Even when we have drawn some kind of line betwen combatants and non-combatants, there remains a further problem, which will be analysed by Miss Anscombe. Granted that we may never deliberately seek to kill an innocent man, must we always refrain from killing combatants if there is a danger of killing non-combatants as well? Clearly not. I may sink an enemy submarine even though I am sure there are prisoners on board. I may destroy an enemy arms dump even if I am sure that nearby civilians will be killed. In such cases I have a definite and justifiable military purpose and it is this that I seek to achieve. I do not deliberately try to kill the non-combatants, their death is a circumstance attendant upon the achieving of my purpose. In the case of combatants, on the other hand, I do *deliberately seek their death as a means* for protecting the community. It seems, then, that I may sometimes take action which issues in the death of non-combatants, provided that their death is *merely a circumstance attendant upon the thing I am trying to do.*

But, clearly, the consequences of an act can be "unintentional" in this sense only (i) if there is a resonable proportion between the intended good and the unintended evil, (ii) if the evil effects do not become too vast in themselves (for there comes a point when sheer scale must deprive the concept of "unintended effects" of meaning), and (iii), above all, if the evil effects do not constitute a foreseen *means* of the good ones (for, of course, if they did, they themselves must needs be intended). And to intend an evil is evil, whatever the ultimate aim: the end does not justify the means.

Thus, suppose that a raid is aimed directly at the houses or hospitals or schools of a city, or is to cover a centre of population so extensively that military and non-military targets are indiscriminately affected, there can no longer be any justification in terms of "double effect". Even if one allowed that the criterion of reasonable proportion might be satisfied; even if one could hold on to the notion of "unintended effects" in view of the massiveness of the circumstances involved: there can be no getting round the fact these evils would be *directly aimed at*. Whatever the ultimate aim (i.e. victory for a just cause), the immediate aim would include the deliberate destruction of non-combatants—would include a commitment to *mass-murder*.

This is why nuclear warfare is immoral. It could hardly achieve a just balance of consequences; and the hugeness of its evils—which, of course might extend to the entire destruction of civilization, grave and permanent harm to future generations, and, potentially, even the total extermination of our species—reduces the notion of "unintended effects" to parody; whilst it is, above all, absolutely clear that its indiscriminate terrors must in fact be directly willed, since "deterrence" ultimately rests on the possibility of "massive retaliation".

Nuclear warfare dramatizes the concept of total war in a uniquely compelling way, though what it dramatizes is not altogether new. Though there are aspects of nuclear war that take it utterly beyond anything man has ever yet afflicted upon himself, there are others that are continuous with previous history. As regards its immediate results, an H-bomb dropped on a city clearly does not differ in principle from, for instance, air-raids in which 100,000 people, including refugees, were killed in a single night. It is simply as if we had stumbled against a mutilated body on our door-step, or had suddenly witnessed an administrative atrocity. Such experiences may rock one into a new alertness—opening one's eyes to things hitherto unnoticed; or they may be neutralized by recalling that, after all, they are not unique. We may see the H-bomb and other atomic weapons as a final revelation of total war— and in the light of this, revise many of our past judgments and tolerances. Or we may swallow this *reductio ad absurdum* for the sake of absurdities swallowed long ago. How often do we hear of the Allies' saturation raids of the last war, or, say, of the behaviour of mercenary armies of the Middle Ages— triumphantly pointed to as brutal and atrocious—as though they were bulls-eye proof of the righteousness of the H-bomb!

3. THE MORALS OF DETERRENCE

Let it be quite clear what we are *not* saying. We are not saying that war can never, in principle, be justified. Nor that there are not powerful motives in justice—and even charity —to protect our countries against communist aggression. We can envisage situations in which, other things being equal, we *ought* to defend our countries—our liberty, our institutions— by force, even at enormous sacrifice. The point is that other things are not equal: their name is "massive nuclear bombardment" and "virtual annihilation".

These names are not of our invention; they are the names, respectively used by the 1958 British Government White Paper on Defence and by President Eisenhower, in his State of the Union Message of 9 January 1958, which—in spite of important modifications, intended to make the "ultimate deterrent" more genuinely *ultimate*—continue to define the basis of

Western defence policy in the Kennedy era. The British White Paper, alluding to "the balancing fears of *mutual annihilation*" (my italics), reaffirms that "the democratic Western nations will never start a war against Russia."

> But it must be well understood that, if Russia were to launch a major attack on them, even with conventional forces only, they would have to hit back with strategic weapons. In fact, the strategy of N.A.T.O. is based on the frank recognition that a full-scale Soviet attack could not be repelled without resort to a *massive nuclear bombardment* of the sources of power in Russia. (My italics.)

And President Eisenhower:

> The most powerful deterrent to war lies in the retaliatory power of our Strategic Air Command and the aircraft of our navy. They present to any potential attacker the prospect of *virtual annihilation* of his own country. Even if we assume a surprise attack on our own bases, our bombers would immediately be on their way in sufficient strength to accomplish this *mission of retaliation*. (My italics.)

One does not need to be a Christian—nor indeed any sort of theist at all—to recognize in these threats a deracination from humanity, and from the humanity within ourselves. But we have the Prophets and the Gospels; and we have a full and precise tradition of the Church's thinking, evolved over the centuries, about the tolerable limits of war. Can it reasonably be claimed that commitments like these do not transgress the traditional limits?

In this tradition, to be reviewed by Roger Smith in Chapter V, there are three principles that have decisive implications in a world of H-bombs:

1. Only just uses of violence may be employed.
2. There must be good hope of success.

3. There must be good hope that the ultimate gains will outweigh the evil effects of the war.

Can it really be supposed that a war of "massive nuclear bombardment", of "virtual annihilation"—of "mutual annihilation"—might somehow be justified in terms of these conditions?[1]

A rhetorical question should never be too sure of itself: there is no doubt that this has been supposed.

For the most part, however, participants in this discussion do not deny the claim that a total nuclear war would be immoral. Instead, those who nevertheless defend the stock-piling of nuclear weapons tend to base themselves on a distinction between "using" and "possessing" these weapons, or between a possible "total war" and the actuality of "nuclear deterrence".

This position is important because of the wide, and at times highly authoritative, support it commands. It will be looked into by Dr. Markus and Mr. Geach in Chapters III and IV. It usually relies on one of three aruguments—or a combination between these arguments—which might be called: (i) the argument from bluff, (ii) the argument from military targets, and (iii) the argument from the enforcement of peace.

(i) *The argument from bluff* simply asserts that, if it came to the point, Western governments would not in fact make good their threats, so that nuclear deterrence does not imply a conditional commitment to total war. Thus it is one thing to "have" these bombs; quite another to "use" them. And, immoral as it may be to engage in total nuclear war, there is nothing immoral about nuclear deterrence.

But are there any grounds at all for assuming that govern-

[1] cf. E. I. Watkins, in *Morals and Missiles*. (Edited by Charles Thompson, 1959).

ments are merely bluffing? (And if there were, would the deterrent be a deterrent?) Was it not, in fact, Western governments who initiated the atomic era with Hiroshima and Nagasaki—and never expressed any regret about these acts? Are we to discount the categorical statements of our statesmen and soldiers, and credit them with the certainty of being liars? And even if it should, in spite of everything, turn out that all this apparatus of bombs and threats was vain, can we, as voters in democratic states, underwrite their commitment to admittedly wicked acts, in the hope, that this commitment might perhaps be dishonoured?

(ii) One must take much more seriously *the argument from military targets*, if only because it is so often taken seriously. It is hardly going too far to suggest that, if this argument had to be withdrawn, the attempt to drive a wedge, morally, between "deterrence" and total war would be fatally impaired. There are several important expositions of this argument. Here I shall rely on an article by Fr. Paul Crane, S.J., from *The Month*, October 1959.[1] The article submits that we cannot assume

that the use of nuclear weapons by a just defendant is necessarily to be identified with the direct massacre of the innocent through the indiscriminate hydrogen bombing of an unjust aggressor's cities and towns. It need not be, for there are now in existence controlled nuclear devices which can be restricted to military targets. At the same time, one can conceive of military targets on which a certain type of nuclear bomb could be used whilst remaining discriminate in its effects: such, for example, could be a fleet at sea. One concludes . . . that nuclear

[1] cf. Dr. L. L. McReavy's formulation in *The Tablet*, 29 March 1958 and the *Clergy Review*, February 1960. These articles are referred to in subsequent chapters. Cf. also "Falconer's" articles, "Should We Disarm?", in *The Catholic Times*, 17 February—10 March 1961

war is not necessarily indiscriminate war and that, in consequence, the use of nuclear weapons by a just defendant is not necessarily immoral.

This argument, it will be noted, does not directly depend on submissions concerning *deterrence*, but on submissions concerning nuclear *warfare* itself. The "wedge", that is, does not seek a point of entry between "deterrence" and actual "use" (it implicitly recognizes that there is here no relevant distinction), but seeks to effect a division within nuclear warfare itself—a division between "controlled", as opposed to "indiscriminate" nuclear war. (On this basis, it is wholly consistent to claim, as Fr. Crane does, that not only "deterrence" but nuclear war itself need not violate the conditions for a just war.)

In a sense this argument is absolutely invulnerable. It is proof against objection, in the same sense in which it would be unobjectionable to assert that the mass-production of pornographic photographs need not necessarily be identified with the direct debauchery of the public, since one can conceive of persons who would find a certain type of pornography of indubitable professional value: such, for example, could be a moral theologian. One certainly might thus conclude that pornography is not necessarily pornographic and that, in consequence, the mass-production of dirty pictures by a patriotic company is not necessarily immoral.

Such arguments are unanswerable. All one can do, perhaps, is to mention a few relevant considerations. One might, for instance, indicate that whilst "controlled nuclear devices" are no doubt very ingenious inventions, it is difficult to restrict governments to controlled nuclear devices. This, one might add, would seem all the more important where governments have in fact categorically proclaimed "to any potential aggres-

sor the prospect of virtual annihilation of his own country".
Then there is that "fleet at sea" (it is remarkable how this
fleet keeps turning up in this connexion): one has to admit,
"a certain type of nuclear bomb" *could* be used against it—
and used with impressive efficiency—whilst remaining discriminate in its effects; though this still leaves the question
how many of these fleets, or armies concentrating in deserts,
perhaps, are likely to be about. What we do, on the other
hand, know with some directness is that many hundreds or
thousands of "a certain type of bomb", and many thousands
or ten-thousands of bombs of other types (not necessarily
negligible) are accumulating in various parts of the globe. We
do know that, already in April 1957, Admiral Burke, United
States Chief of Naval Operations, felt confident that "enough
nuclear weapons for 'complete destruction' of the Soviet
Union" were available in the United States.[1] And we do
know that American civil defence specialists have found it
convenient to give a new word—a unit—to our language:
"megacorpse": one million dead bodies. . . .

Moral theologians concerned to fence off criticisms of
nuclear weapons may choose to affirm theoretical possibilities
no longer found relevant by strategists, statesmen or common
sense, but it is time to match gravity with gravity. Pope
John XXIII, in his encyclical *Ad Petri Cathedrum*, of June
1959, chose to speak not of how one might still "conceive"
of "military targets", of fleets at sea, of a nuclear war "not
necessarily indiscriminate", but of the dangers of "drifting"

in utter blindness towards a new and frightful war. In utter
blindness, we say, for if indeed (which may God avert!) a new
war should break out, the power of the monstrous new weapons
is such that all the nations, victors and vanquished alike, would

[1] Philip Noel-Baker, *The Arms Race*, p. 174.

be left with nothing but a scene of universal ruin and destruction.[1]

(iii) The last of these three arguments, *the argument from the enforcement of peace,* is sometimes associated with one or the other, or both, of the preceding arguments, sometimes it is offered by itself. It is the most popular of all these arguments, being also the standard *secular* apologia for "deterrence": it is, for instance, the basis of Mr. Gaitskell's plea that deterrence is in accordance with "principle". Rightly or wrongly, the maintenance of "the deterrent" is thus held to be not only necessary for Western defence but necessary for present peace —as also for the establishment of international arrangements that would secure the peace of the future.

In its own terms, this is a strong argument; though, as we have already had occasion to note, even on the plane of expediency, there are powerful arguments to place against it. But even if, for discussion's sake, we assume that, on balance, the deterrent may support peace, this would not necessarily justify it. It would justify it *if, and only if, in employing this threat, we were not already involved in immoral risks —and in immoral hypothetical decisions.* The two preceding arguments purport precisely to meet this condition; they are meant to demonstrate that no evil *need* attach to the threat of nuclear war. If this could indeed be shown, then the goods of security and peace might undoubtedly justify the maintenance of the deterrent—and indeed might oblige us to maintain it. As we have seen (and as Chapter III will demonstrate in detail), the arguments fail to support their claims. And nothing, not even the alleged interests of peace itself, can save murderousness from evil.

[1] cf. Ch. V for fuller extracts from this and other relevant Papal statements.

4. A "NECESSARY EVIL"?

In the end, however, the discussion may shift to another plane. Sooner or later, someone will return to the plea that we simply have *no choice*. If nuclear deterrence is evil, it is a necessary evil; it is the lesser of the two evils confronting us. What could be a greater evil than to be conquered by communism—not only to lose our liberties and suffer persecution but to see our children exposed to this immensely efficient parody of Faith?

This argument has the dignity of speaking with the voice with which it thinks. And it matches the gravity of the challenge we are facing. It is, moreover, an argument that probes deeply into our ultimate commitments. It is conscious that behind the phrase "the defence of the West" lies a meaning more deep-seated than any connected with military strategy. And in this awareness, it exposes itself to real questions.

One might, for instance, consider once more whether the potential destruction of mankind is indeed so surely a "lesser evil" than a military triumph of communism. If we are liberal humanists, we might ask ourselves just how deeply we believe in man. If we are Christians, we might take this opportunity to reconsider what it is we believe.

And we could check on that potently ambiguous phrase "no choice". Do we mean that there literally is *no alternative* to this course? Or do we mean that we have *lost our freedom to choose*? Or do we actually mean to claim, with some part of our minds, that a decision to do without the evil of nuclear "defence" would be so *morally* outrageous as to be unthinkable?

We are thus finally led to ask whether, when we speak in this way of "necessary evils", we are not doing more from within to harm what we defend than any enemy could do from outside. The word "evil" can, of course, be used in either a moral or a non-moral sense; and it is disastrously easy to slip from one sense into the other, especially when speaking of "necessary evils". We may say, for instance, that—in certain situations—war may be a necessary evil. This can only mean that, though intrinsically *dreadful*, war may sometimes be the lesser of two dreadful things. For to be the lesser of two evils, it must certainly be *morally* good, or at least avoid being morally evil: since, whatever is *morally evil* is *ipso facto* absolutely to be dreaded. A "necessary evil" can thus only be evil in a non-moral sense. Yet again and again people slip into ways of speaking which assume that "necessary evils" may include necessary *moral* evils, so that the choice between two evils may be a choice between two morally repugnant rescources.

This fallacy is, unfortunately, much more than logical. For to regard a "necessary evil" as the lesser of two *moral* evils is, quite literally, to surrender to evil. It assumes a world that is morally self-contradictory, a world that obliges one to morally evil acts. And, in assuming such a world, it ensures that one's choices will actually be evil choices.

It ensures this by obliterating any sense of moral road-blocks. Where everything is tainted with moral evil, nothing is absolutely barred. Once you believe that wickedness can be forced upon you, not because of your cowardice or human weakness but because of the way the world is, then morality is shifted to another world. "In an ideal world, no doubt, it would be possible to observe absolute prohibitions of such things as the murder of children, but of course in the real world these things can be forced upon us." This kind of moral sell-out is, of course, commonly masked by high-sounding phrases. Often these are variations on the theme of "realism" and common sense. Or men who simply suffer from panic can pose as tragic heroes driven to evil by forces outside their control. They believe that they are "morally earnest"—almost conscientious objectors to conscience—because they have a certain nostalgia for the ideal world. They can even fool themselves into thinking that they are bringing it into being —that their habitual moral squalor is the price they must pay for the well-being of future generations. They are, in fact, earnestly devoted to the happiness of the human race—to what James Joyce used to characterize as securing "as cheaply as possible the greatest possible happiness of the greatest possible number". Surely, they think, it cannot be *their* fault if the price is at times a bit stiff.

Sometimes it is stiffer than others. No communist, these days, would hesitate to admit that it was occasionally rather high during the progress of the Soviet Union, and that— fascists or no fascists—the necessity for that Hungarian business was—well, a pity. Germans, today, are mostly agreed that the necessities associated with the Third Reich were ill-founded and immoderate. Americans and Englishmen are outraged by developments in South Africa—made necessary in defence of Western civilization—and, similarly, often doubt whether some French methods in Algeria can have been as necessary as all that. Yet the moral price paid by the Allies in Hiroshima and Nagasaki is still widely accepted as a statesmanlike, courageous act (did it not help to shorten the war?); so that the ultimate reduction to bloody licence we have ever since lived with is taken for granted as just another "necessary evil".

But the fact is, the H-bomb is calling our bluff. The *defence of the West*, it seems to ask. What West? The West of the rationalist movement that gave birth to Marxist thought and now seems distinguishable from its offspring only by its lingering inconsistencies? Or the West of a Christianity so thin as to have called down upon its world the revolt of the betrayed, and that now protests it has no choice but to do evil to prevent evil?

It is comforting to turn to Pope Pius XII's address to the World Medical Association of 30 September 1954, on A.B.C. —atomic, biological and chemical—warfare. His words have an importance not yet generally understood:

> Should the evil consequences of adopting this method of warfare ever become so extensive as to pass utterly beyond the control of man, then indeed its use must be rejected as immoral. In that event, it would no longer be a question of "defence" against injustice and necessary "protection" of legitimate possessions, but of the annihilation, pure and simple, of all human life within the affected area. That is not lawful on any title.[1]

It is true that there are other Papal statements stressing nations' continued right to self-defence against aggression; and the total implications of Pope Pius XII's varying emphases may be open to dispute.[2] But nothing can alter the force of the sentence: "Should the evil consequences of adopting this method of warfare ever become so extensive as to pass utterly beyond the control of man, then its use must be rejected as immoral". The passage as a whole does not, of course, preclude the need for further analysis and definition: it does not imply that anything *short* of "utterly beyond the control of man" would necessarily be lawful. It simply reaffirms, in the context of our extreme predicament, the Church's constant, historic affirmation that there are *limits*—creaturely limits, in war as in every other sphere of human action; that these limits bind, and sustain, us even in the face of the most urgent "necessity"; that there are no "necessary" moral evils.

[1] *Acta Apostolicæ Sedis*, xxxxvi-II-xxi, p. 587 ss.
[2] cf. Chapter V.

In the normal run of the world, force is a right and necessary condition of order and humane existence. We cannot imagine a world that would not, man being what he is, require a measure of physical power, to restrain abuses of physical power. Till the end of history, there will be a place for armed restraint of aggression. And in times of ideological crisis like ours, the capacity to restrain is, of course, quite especially important. Yet it is precisely at this moment of extreme need for physical protection that effective physical force seems to elude us, beyond its ultimate tolerable limits.

Even so—even as we look back on the annunciations of Christmas Island, or celebrate satellite epiphanies—there is this to hold on to: A policy of unconditional disarmament could break through the closed circle of terror within which we coexist. It could form the basis of reciprocal disarmament without illusions. It could free our resources to fight world-poverty and world-resentment. Should we, however, be invaded, there is the ultimate weapon of meaningful suffering. "If we believe we should defend our civilization and our way of life, then we should be prepared to defend it at whatever the cost."

At the root of our civilization there are, after all, sources of hope and resources of defence proof against every human contingency. Heaven and earth will pass away, but no "necessity", however extreme, can divorce us from these sources: whatever the cost, there is, after all, only one thing necessary in the end.

II

WAR AND MURDER

G. E. M. Anscombe

1. THE USE OF VIOLENCE BY RULERS

Since there are always thieves and frauds and men who commit violent attacks on their neighbours and murderers, and since without law backed by adequate force there are usually gangs of bandits; and since there are in most places laws administered by people who command violence to enforce the laws against law-breakers; the question arises: what is a just attitude to this exercise of violent coercive power on the part of rulers and their subordinate officers?

Two attitudes are possible: one, that the world is an absolute jungle and that the exercise of coercive power by rulers is only a manifestation of this; and the other, that it is both necessary and right that there should be this exercise of power, that through it the world is much less of a jungle than it could possibly be without it, so that one should in principle be glad of the existence of such power, and only take exception to its unjust exercise.

It is so clear that the world is less of a jungle because of rulers and laws, and that the exercise of coercive power is essential to these institutions as they are now—all this is so obvious, that probably only Tennysonian conceptions of progress enable people who do not wish to separate themselves from the world to think that nevertheless such violence is objectionable, that some day, in this present dispensation, we shall do without it, and that the pacifist is the man who sees and tries to follow the ideal course, which future civilization must one day pursue. It is an illusion, which would be fantastic if it were not so familiar.

In a peaceful and law abiding country such as England, it may not be immediately obvious that the rulers need to command violence to the point of fighting to the death those that would oppose it; but brief reflection shews that this is so. For those who oppose the force that backs law will not always stop short of fighting to the death and cannot always be put down short of fighting to the death.

Then only if it is in itself evil violently to coerce resistant wills, can the exercise of coercive power by rulers be bad as such. Against such a conception, if it were true, the necessity and advantage of the exercise of such power would indeed be a useless plea. But that conception is one that makes no sense unless it is accompanied by a theory of withdrawal from the world as man's only salvation; and it is in any case a false one. We are taught that God retains the evil will of the devil within limits by violence: we are not given a picture of God permitting to the devil all that he is capable of. There is current a conception of Christianity as having revealed that the defeat of evil must always be by pure love without coercion; this at least is shewn to be false by the foregoing consideration. And without the alleged revelation there could be no reason to believe such a thing.

To think that society's coercive authority is evil is akin to thinking the flesh evil and family life evil. These things belong to the present constitution of mankind; and if the exercise of coercive power is a manifestation of evil, and not the just means of restraining it, then human nature is totally depraved in a manner never taught by Christianity. For society is essential to human good; and society without coercive power is generally impossible .

The same authority which puts down internal dissension, which promulgates laws and restrains those who break them if it can, must equally oppose external enemies. These do not merely comprise those who attack the borders of the people ruled by the authority; but also, for example, pirates and desert bandits, and, generally, those beyond the confines of the country ruled whose activities are viciously harmful to it. The Romans, once their rule in Gaul was established, were eminently justified in attacking Britain, where were nurtured the Druids whose pupils infested northern Gaul and whose practices struck the Romans themselves as "dira immanitas". Further, there being such a thing as the common good of mankind, and visible criminality against it, how can we doubt the excellence of such a proceeding as that violent suppression of the man-stealing business[1] which the British government took it into its head to engage in under Palmerston? The present-day conception of "aggression", like so many strongly influential conceptions, is a bad one. Why *must* it be wrong to strike the first blow in a struggle? The only question is, who is in the right.

Here, however, human pride, malice and cruelty are so usual that it is true to say that wars have mostly been mere wickedness on both sides. Just as an individual will constantly think himself in the right, whatever he does, and yet there is still such a thing as being in the right, so nations will constantly wrongly think themselves to be in the right—and yet there is still such a thing as their being in the right. Palmerston doubtless had no doubts in prosecuting the opium war against China, which was diabolical; just as he exulted

[1] It is ignorance to suppose that it takes modern liberalism to hate and condemn this. It is cursed and subject to the death penalty in the Mosiac law. Under that code, too, runaway slaves of all nations had asylum in Israel.

in putting down the slavers. But there is no question but that he was a monster in the one thing, and a just man in the other.

The probability is that warfare is injustice, that a life of military service is a bad life "militia or rather malitia," as St. Anselm called it. This probability is greater than the probability (which also exists) that membership of a police force will involve malice, because of the character of warfare: the extraordinary occasions it offers for viciously unjust proceedings on the part of military commanders and warring governments, which at the time attract praise and not blame from their people. It is equally the case that the life of a ruler is usually a vicious life: but that does not shew that ruling is as such a vicious activity.

The principal wickedness which is a temptation to those engaged in warfare is the killing of the innocent, which may often be done with impunity and even to the glory of those who do it. In many places and times it has been taken for granted as a natural part of waging war: the commander, and especially the conqueror, massacres people by the thousand, either because this is part of his glory, or as a terrorizing measure, or as part of his tactics .

2. INNOCENCE AND THE RIGHT TO KILL INTENTIONALLY

It is necessary to dwell on the notion of non-innocence here employed. Innocence is a legal notion; but here, the accused is not pronounced guilty under an existing code of law, under which he has been tried by an impartial judge, and therefore made the target of attack. There is hardly a possibility of this; for the administration of justice is something that takes place under the aegis of a sovereign authority; but in warfare—or

48

the putting down by violence of civil disturbance—the sovereign authority is itself engaged as a party to the dispute and is not subject to a further earthly and temporal authority which can judge the issue and pronounce against the accused. The stabler the society, the rarer it will be for the sovereign authority to have to do anything but apprehend its internal enemy and have him tried; but even in the stablest society there are occasions when the authority has to fight its internal enemy to the point of killing, as happens in the struggle with external belligerent forces in international warfare; and then the characterization of its enemy as non-innocent has not been ratified by legal process.

This, however, does not mean that the notion of innocence fails in this situation. What is required, for the people attacked to be non-innocent in the relevant sense, is that they should themselves be engaged in an objectively unjust proceeding which the attacker has the right to make his concern; or—the commonest case—should be unjustly attacking him. Then he can attack them with a view to stopping them; and also their supply lines and armament factories. But people whose mere existence and activity supporting existence by growing crops, making clothes, etc. constitute an impediment to him—such people are innocent and it is murderous to attack them, or make them a target for an attack which he judges will help him towards victory. For murder is the deliberate killing of the innocent, whether for its own sake or as a means to some further end.

The right to attack with a view to killing is something that belongs only to rulers and those whom they command to do it. I have argued that it does belong to rulers precisely because of that threat of violent coercion exercised by those in authority which is essential to the existence of human societies. It ought not to be pretended that rulers and their subordinates do not choose[1] the killing of their enemies as a means, when it has come to fighting in which they are determined to win and their enemies resist to the point of killing: this holds even in internal disturbances.

When a private man struggles with an enemy he has no right to aim to kill him, unless in the circumstances of the attack on him he can be considered as endowed with the authority of the law and the struggle comes to that point. By a "private" man, I mean a man in a society; I am not speaking of men on their own, without government, in remote places; for such men are neither public servants nor "private". The plea of self-defence (or the defence of someone else) made by a private man who has killed someone else must in conscience—even if not in law—be a plea that the death of the other was not intended, but was a side effect of the measures taken to ward off the attack. To shoot to kill, to set lethal man-traps, or, say, to lay poison for someone from whom one's life is in danger, are forbidden. The deliberate choice of inflicting death in a struggle is the right only of ruling authorities and their subordinates.

In saying that a private man may not choose to kill, we are touching on the principle of "double effect". The denial of this has been the corruption of non-Catholic thought, and its abuse the corruption of Catholic thought. Both have disastrous consequences which we shall see. This principle is not accepted in English law: the law is said to allow no distinction between the foreseen and the intended consequences of an action. Thus, if I push a man over a cliff when he is menac-

---

[1] The idea that they may lawfully do what they do, but should not *intend* the death of those they attack, has been put forward and, when suitably expressed, may seem high-minded. But someone who can fool himself into this twist of thought will fool himself into justifying anything, however atrocious, by means of it.

ing my life, his death is considered as intended by me, but the intention to be justifiable for the sake of self-defence. Yet the lawyers would hardly find the laying of poison tolerable as an act of self-defence, but only killing by a violent action in a moment of violence. Christian moral theologians have taught that even here one may not seek the death of the assailant, but may in default of other ways of self-defence use such violence as will in fact result in his death. The distinction is evidently a fine one in some cases: what, it may be asked, can the intention be, if it can be said to be absent in this case, except a mere wish or desire?

And yet in other cases the distinction is very clear. If I go to prison rather than perform some action, no reasonable person will call the incidental consequences of my refusal—the loss of my job, for example—intentional just because I knew they must happen. And in the case of the administration of a pain-relieving drug in mortal illness, where the doctor knows the drug may very well kill the patient if the illness does not do so first, the distinction is evident; the lack of it has led an English judge to talk nonsense about the administration of the drug's not having *really* been the cause of death in such a case, even though a post mortem shews it was. For everyone understands that it is a very different thing so to administer a drug, and to administer it with the intention of killing. However, the principle of double effect has more important applications in warfare, and I shall return to it later.

3. THE INFLUENCE OF PACIFISM

Pacifism has existed as a considerable movement in English speaking countries ever since the first world war. I take the doctrine of pacifism to be that it is *eo ipso* wrong to fight in wars, not the doctrine that it is wrong to be compelled to, or that any man, or some men, may refuse; and I think it false for the reasons that I have given. But I now want to consider the very remarkable effects it has had: for I believe its influence to have been enormous, far exceeding its influence on its own adherents.

We should note first that pacifism has as its background conscription and enforced military service for all men. Without conscription, pacifism is a private opinion that will keep those who hold it out of armies, which they are in any case not obliged to join. Now universal conscription, except for the most extraordinary reasons, i.e. as a regular habit among most nations, is such a horrid evil that the refusal of it automatically commands a certain amount of respect and sympathy.

We are not here concerned with the pacifism of some peculiar sect which in any case draws apart from the world to a certain extent, but with a pacifism of people in the world, who do not want to be withdrawn from it. For some of these, pacifism is prevented from being a merely theoretical attitude because they are liable to, and so are prepared to resist conscription; or are able directly to effect the attitude of some who are so liable.

A powerful ingredient in this pacifism is the prevailing image of Christianity. This image commands a sentimental respect among people who have no belief in Christianity, that is to say, in Christian dogmas; yet do have a certain belief in an ideal which they conceive to be part of "true Christianity". It is therefore important to understand this image of Christianity and to know how false it is. Such understanding is relevant, not merely to those who wish to believe Christianity, but to all who, without the least wish to believe, are yet profoundly influenced by this image of it.

According to this image, Christianity is an ideal and beautiful religion, impracticable except for a few rare characters. It preaches a God of love whom there is no reason to fear; it marks an escape from the conception presented in the Old Testament, of a vindictive and jealous God who will terribly punish his enemies. The "Christian" God is a *roi fainéant*, whose only triumph is in the Cross; his appeal is to goodness and unselfishness, and to follow him is to act according to the Sermon on the Mount—to turn the other cheek and to offer no resistance to evil. In this account some of the evangelical counsels are chosen as containing the whole of Christian ethics: that is, they are made into precepts. (Only some of them; it is not likely that someone who deduces the *duty* of pacifism from the Sermon on the Mount and the rebuke to Peter, will agree to take "Give to him that asks of you" equally as a universally binding precept.)

The turning of counsels into precepts results in high-sounding principles. Principles that are mistakenly high and strict are a trap; they may easily lead in the end directly or indirectly to the justification of monstrous things. Thus if the evangelical counsel about poverty were turned into a precept forbidding property owning, people would pay lip service to it as the ideal, while in practice they went in for swindling. "Absolute honesty!" it would be said: "I can respect that —but of course that means having no property; and while I respect those who follow that course, I have to compromise with the sordid world myself." If then one must "compromise with evil" by owning property and engaging in trade, then the amount of swindling one does will depend on convenience. This imaginary case is paralleled by what is so commonly said: absolute pacifism is an ideal; unable to follow that, and committed to "compromise with evil", one must go the whole hog and wage war *à outrance*.

The truth about Christianity is that it is a severe and practicable religion, not a beautifully ideal but impracticable one.

Its moral precepts, (except for the stricter laws about marriage that Christ enacted, abrogating some of the permissions of the Old Law) are those of the Old Testament; and its God is the God of Israel.

It is ignorance of the New Testament that hides this from people. It is characteristic of pacifism to denigrate the Old Testament and exalt the New: something quite contrary to the teaching of the New Testament itself, which always looks back to and leans upon the Old. How typical it is that the words of Christ "You have heard it said, an eye for an eye and a tooth for a tooth, but I say to you . . ." are taken as a repudiation of the ethic of the Old Testament! People seldom look up the occurrence of this phrase in the juridical code of the Old Testament, where it belongs, and is the admirable principle of law for the punishment of certain crimes, such as procuring the wrongful punishment of another by perjury. People often enough *now* cite the phrase to justify private revenge; no doubt this was as often "heard said" when Christ spoke of it. But no justification for this exists in the personal ethic taught by the Old Testament. On the contrary. What do we find? "Seek no revenge," (Leviticus xix, 18), and "If you find your enemy's ox or ass going astray, take it back to him; if you see the ass of someone who hates you lying under his burden, and would forbear to help him: you must help him" (Exodus xxiii, 4-5). And "If your enemy is hungry, give him food, if thirsty, give him drink" (Proverbs xxv, 21).

This is only one example; given space, it would be easy to shew how false is the conception of Christ's teaching as *correcting* the religion of the ancient Israelites, and substituting a higher and more "spiritual" religion for theirs. Now the false picture I have described plays an important part in the pacifist ethic and in the ethic of the many people who are not pacifists but are influenced by pacifism.

To extract a pacifist doctrine—i.e. a condemnation of the use of force by the ruling authorities, and of soldiering as a profession—from the evangelical counsels and the rebuke to Peter, is to disregard what else is in the New Testament. It is to forget St. John's direction to soldiers: "do not blackmail people; be content with your pay"; and Christ's commendation of the centurion, who compared his authority over his men to Christ's. On a pacifist view, this must be much as if a madam in a brothel had said: "I know what authority is, I tell this girl to do this, and she does it . . ." and Christ had commended her faith. A centurion was the first Gentile to be baptized; there is no suggestion in the New Testament that soldiering was regarded as incompatible with Christianity. The martyrology contains many names of soldiers whose occasion for martyrdom was not any objection to soldiering, but a refusal to perform idolatrous acts.

Now, it is one of the most vehement and repeated teachings of the Judaeo-Christian tradition that the shedding of innocent blood is forbidden by the divine law. No man may be punished except for his own crime, and those "whose feet are swift to shed innocent blood" are always represented as God's enemies.

For a long time the main outlines of this teaching have seemed to be merely obvious morality: hence, for example, I have read a passage by Ronald Knox complaining of the "endless moralizing", interspersed in records of meanness, cowardice, spite, cruelty, treachery and murder, which forms so much of the Old Testament. And indeed, that it is terrible to kill the innocent is very obvious; the morality that so stringently forbids it must make a great appeal to mankind, especially to the poor threatened victims. Why should it need the thunder of Sinai and the suffering and preaching of the prophets to promulgate such a law? But human pride and malice are everywhere so strong that now, with the fading of Christianity from the mind of the West, this morality once more stands out as a demand which strikes pride-and fear-ridden people as too intransigent. For Knox, it seemed so obvious as to be dull; and he failed to recognize the bloody and beastly records that it accompanies for the dry truthfulness about human beings that so characterizes the Old Testament.[1]

Now pacifism teaches people to make no distinction between the shedding of innocent blood and the shedding of any human blood. And in this way pacifism has corrupted enormous numbers of people who will not act according to its tenets. They become convinced that a number of things are wicked which are not; hence, seeing no way of avoiding "wickedness", they set no limits to it. How endlessly pacifists argue that all war must be à outrance! that those who wage war must go as far as technological advance permits in the destruction of the enemy's people. As if the Napoleonic wars were perforce fuller of massacres than the French war of Henry V of England. It is not true: the reverse took place. Nor is technological advance particularly relevant; it is mere squeamishness that deters people who would consent to area bombing from the enormous massacres by hand that used once to be committed.

The policy of obliterating cities was adopted by the Allies in the last war; they need not have taken that step, and it was taken largely out of a villainous hatred, and as corollary to the policy, now universally denigrated, of seeking "uncondi-

[1] It is perhaps necessary to remark that I am not here adverting to the total extermination of certain named tribes of Canaan that is said by the Old Testament to have been commanded by God. That is something quite outside the provisions of the Mosaic Law for dealings in war.

56

tional surrender". (That policy itself was visibly wicked, and could be and was judged so at the time; it is not surprising that it led to disastrous consequences, even if no one was clever and detached enough to foresee this at the time.)

Pacifism and the respect for pacifism is not the only thing that has led to a universal forgetfulness of the law against killing the innocent; but it has had a great share in it.

4. THE PRINCIPLE OF DOUBLE EFFECT

Catholics, however, can hardly avoid paying at least lip-service to that law. So we must ask: how is it that there has been so comparatively little conscience exercised on the subject among them? The answer is: double-think about double effect.

The distinction between the intended, and the merely foreseen, effects of a voluntary action is indeed absolutely essential to Christian ethics. For Christianity forbids a number of things as being bad in themselves. But if I am answerable for the foreseen consequences of an action or refusal, as much as for the action itself, then these prohibitions will break down. If someone innocent will die unless I do a wicked thing, then on this view I am his murderer in refusing: so all that is left to me is to weigh up evils. Here the theologian steps in with the principle of double effect and says: "No, you are no murderer, if the man's death was neither your aim nor your chosen means, and if you had to act in the way that led to it or else do something absolutely forbidden". Without understanding of this principle, anything can be—and is wont to be—justified, and the Christian teaching that in no circumstances may one commit murder, adultery, apostasy (to give a few examples) goes by the board. These absolute prohibitions of Christianity by no means exhaust its ethic; there is a large area where what is just is determined partly by a prudent

weighing up of consequences. But the prohibitions are bed-
rock, and without them the Christian ethic goes to pieces.
Hence the necessity of the notion of double effect.

At the same time, the principle has been repeatedly abused
from the seventeenth century up till now. The causes lie in
the history of philosophy. From the seventeenth century till
now what may be called Cartesian psychology has dominated
the thought of philosophers and theologians. According to this
psychology, an intention was an interior act of the mind which
could be produced at will. Now if intention is all important
—as it is—in determining the goodness or badness of an action,
then, on this theory of what intention is, a marvellous way
offered itself of making any action lawful. You only had to
"direct your intention" in a suitable way. In practice, this
means making a little speech to yourself: "What I mean to be
doing is. . . ."

This perverse doctrine has occasioned repeated condemna-
tions by the Holy See from the seventeenth century to the
present day. Some examples will suffice to shew how the thing
goes. Typical doctrines from the seventeenth century were
that it is all right for a servant to hold the ladder for his
criminous master so long as he is merely avoiding the sack by
doing so; or that a man might wish for and rejoice at his
parent's death so long as what he had in mind was the gain
to himself; or that it is not simony to offer money, not *as a
price* for the spiritual benefit, but only *as an inducement*
to give it. A condemned doctrine from the present day is
that the practice of *coitus reservatus* is permissable: such a
doctrine could only arise in connexion with that "direction
of intention" which sets everything right no matter what
one does. A man makes a practice of withdrawing, telling
himself that he *intends* not to ejaculate; of course (if that
is his practice) he usually does so, but then the event is

58

"accidental" and *praeter intentionem*: it is, in short, a case of "double effect."

This same doctrine is used to prevent any doubts about the obliteration bombing of a city. The devout Catholic bomber secures by a "direction of intention" that any shedding of innocent blood that occurs is "accidental". I know a Catholic boy who was puzzled at being told by his schoolmaster that it was an *accident* that the people of Hiroshima and Nagasaki were there to be killed; in fact, however absurd it seems, such thoughts are common among priests who know that they are forbidden by the divine law to justify the direct killing of the innocent.

It is nonsense to pretend that you do not intend to do what is the means you take to your chosen end. Otherwise there is absolutely no substance to the Pauline teaching that we may not do evil that good may come.

5. SOME COMMONLY HEARD ARGUMENTS

There are a number of sophistical arguments, often or sometimes used on these topics, which need answering.

Where do you draw the line? As Dr. Johnson said, the fact of twilight does not mean you cannot tell day from night. There are borderline cases, where it is difficult to distinguish, in what is done, between means and what is incidental to, yet in the circumstances inseparable from, those means. The obliteration bombing of a city is not a borderline case.

The old "conditions for a just war" are irrelevant to the conditions of modern warfare, so that must be condemned out of hand. People who say this always envisage only major wars between the Great Powers, which Powers are indeed now "in blood stepp'd in so far" that it is unimaginable for there to be a war between them which is not a set of enormous massacres of civil populations. But these are not the only wars.

Why is Finland so far free? At least partly because of the "posture of military preparedness" which, considering the character of the country, would have made subjugating the Finns a difficult and unrewarding task. The offensive of the Israelis against the Egyptians in 1956 involved no plan of making civil populations the target of military attack.

In a modern war the distinction between combatants and non-combatants is meaningless, so an attack on anyone on the enemy side is justified. This is pure nonsense; even in war, a very large number of the enemy population are just engaged in maintaining the life of the country, or are sick, or aged, or children.

It must be legitimate to maintain an opinion—viz. that the destruction of cities by bombing is lawful—if this is argued by competent theologians and the Holy See has not pronounced. The argument from the silence of the Holy See has itself been condemned by the Holy See (Denzinger, 28th Edition, 1127). How could this be a sane doctrine in view of the endless twistiness of the human mind?

Whether a war is just or not is not for the private man to judge: he must obey his government. Sometimes, this may be, especially as far as concerns causes of war. But the individual who joins in destroying a city, like a Nazi massacring the inhabitants of a village, is too obviously marked out as an enemy of the human race, to shelter behind such a plea.

Finally, horrible as it is to have to notice this, we must notice that even the arguments about double effect—which at least show that a man is not willing openly to justify the killing of the innocent—are now beginning to look old-fashioned. Some Catholics are not scrupling to say that *anything* is justified in defence of the continued existence and liberty of the Church in the West. A terrible fear of communism drives people to say this sort of thing. "Our Lord told us to fear those who can destroy body and soul, not to fear the destruction of the body" was blasphemously said to a friend of mine; meaning: "so, we must fear Russian domination more than the destruction of people's bodies by obliteration bombing".

But whom did Our Lord tell us to fear, when he said: "I will tell you whom you shall fear" and "Fear not them that can destroy the body, but fear him who can destroy body and soul in hell"? He told us to fear God the Father, who can and will destroy the unrepentant disobedient, body and soul, in hell.

A Catholic who is tempted to think on the lines I have described should remember that the Church is the spiritual Israel: that is, that Catholics are what the ancient Jews were, salt for the earth and the people of God—and that what was true of some devout Jews of ancient times can equally well be true of us now: "You compass land and sea to make a convert, and when you have done so, you make him twice as much a child of hell as yourselves". Do Catholics sometimes think that they are immune from such a possibility? That the Pharisees—who sat in the seat of Moses and who were so zealous for the true religion—were bad in ways in which we cannot be bad if we are zealous? I believe they do. But our faith teaches no such immunity, it teaches the opposite. "We are in danger all our lives long". So we have to fear God and keep his commandments, and calculate what is for the best only within the limits of that obedience, knowing that the future is in God's power and that no one can snatch away those whom the Father has given to Christ.

It is not a vague faith in the triumph of "the spirit" over force (there is little enough warrant for that), but a definite faith in the divine promises, that makes us believe that the Church cannot fail. Those, therefore, who think they must be prepared to wage a war with Russia involving the deliberate massacre of cities, must be prepared to say to God: "We had to break your law, lest your Church fail. We could not obey your commandments, for we did not believe your promises."

III

CONSCIENCE AND DETERRENCE

R. A. Markus

THINGS ARE not in themselves evil, and nuclear weapons are no exception to this truism. It is the use to which we put things that may or may not be evil. In discussing the morality of nuclear weapons, their use in warfare, their possession and manufacture in peace-time, their use as a means of foreign policy, and so forth, we are discussing the morality of human actions. In having shown that nuclear war obliterates the distinction between civilians and combatants and therefore involves the deliberate taking of innocent life, that is to say, murder, we have only begun to answer the moral questions which they raise for us. We have in fact answered only the first question: we have found that if we use nuclear weapons for the purpose they are by their nature fitted for, that is to say, for large-scale and indiscriminate destruction, then we are simply guilty of mass-murder. But is this the only manner in which they can be used? Are there not other ways and other purposes, particular circumstances, which may make the use of nuclear weapons a legitimate means of waging war?

In this chapter we shall attempt to answer questions such as these. We may group them under the following three headings:

1. Are there possible *special circumstances* in which nuclear weapons could legitimately be used?

2. Is *possession* of nuclear weapons legitimate, particularly if there are grounds for hoping that by possessing them we shall be able to avoid having to use them?

3. What *practical consequences*, individual and collective decisions, should follow from the answers to these questions?

1. USE OF NUCLEAR WEAPONS IN SPECIAL CIRCUMSTANCES

Many of those who hold that the use of nuclear weapons is not normally permissable would nevertheless except certain special circumstances, in which, they would urge, no moral blame attaches to using them. We may again distinguish three positions here and deal with them one by one.

(i) *In self-defence against communism*

It is sometimes held that although nuclear warfare is morally evil, totalitarian communism is, however, a "greater evil", and that in self-defence against so great an evil it is morally justifiable to have recourse to nuclear warfare. We know that our enemy is unlikely to be inhibited by such moral scruples; why not seize our only chance of effective defence?

Little need be said about this argument because this, like the next one to be discussed in a moment, has in fact been fully met in the previous chapters. People who argue like this have in fact not seen the *moral* case against nuclear warfare. They may regard it as a "bad thing", a thing to be avoided if at all possible; but they have failed to see that it is morally inadmissable. To see this means to see that we are not permitted to murder even if murder offers the only chance of our defending what we hold valuable above all things.

(ii) *In retaliation against an aggressor already using nuclear weapons*

Equally little need be said—the same remark would suffice

—about another set of circumstances which are sometimes held to justify recourse to nuclear war, namely in retaliation or in self-defence against an aggressor already using nuclear weapons. Thus, for instance, *The Tablet* has frequently declared that it is hard to understand how any one can claim that there is a moral justification for using these weapons against an enemy who has not used them first. But should it be less hard to understand how any one can claim that there is a moral justification for committing a crime when someone else has committed one first? A crime is a crime, no matter who commits it first, and what the "extenuating circumstances".

It may be deplorable to set an example of crime in a world only too ready to exploit and follow such example, it is always regrettable to be the first to commit a crime; just as it is laudable to be the first to do good. But the former is "regrettable" and the latter laudable, above all, because the act is in one case evil, in the other good.

(iii) *Against restricted targets.*

We have to take more seriously a third set of circumstances in which, it has been suggested, nuclear weapons may be used without incurring the guilt of murder. Such, it has been urged, would be the case with large concentrations of enemy forces sufficiently isolated to make it possible to use nuclear weapons discriminatingly against them without destroying civilian populations. An argument of this type has been well put by Dr. L. L. McReavy in an article in *The Tablet*[1] as well as in the course of a later article in the *Clergy Review*,[2] other aspects of which are also discussed by Mr. P. T. Geach in Chapter IV below. Dr. McReavy denies that "a predominantly

[1] 29 March 1958.
[2] "The Debate on the Morality of Future War", February 1960.

civilian town can ever be a legitimate target for so indiscriminate a weapon as a nuclear bomb, without first abandoning the principles of morality in self-defence and substituting the principle of expediency". He goes on to insist that "in no circumstances, not even to save the Western world from being swamped by communism" could such actions be justified. Deliberate killing of the innocent remains murder, no matter why one does it or who starts it first. But, Dr. McReavy suggests, "at least in theory there can be legitimate targets even for the major nuclear weapons (e.g. a large hostile force, conveniently, if improbably, concentrated)"; and therefore the State "is morally entitled to construct such weapons as deterrents, and indeed to test their efficacy, unless the genetic risks of such tests outweigh their utility".

We are not here concerned with the genetic hazards of testing nuclear devices at all; and we shall discuss later (in section 2) questions about the morality of using nuclear weapons for deterrence. Let us agree at once that it is possible to think up such cases, in which the use of nuclear weapons is not necessarily immoral. We add here in passing that there may be scope for the use of smaller ("tactical") atomic weapons with sufficient discrimination not to incur moral reprehension. We may concede that it is legitimate to manufacture and hold supplies of nuclear weapons *for this purpose*; but does this mean that we may acquiesce in the manufacture and stockpiling of nuclear weapons of all sizes, without any kind of reassurance about their purpose?

Dr. McReavy himself reminds us that "the conditions for a legitimate kind of use are unlikely of fulfilment"; "there are very few [targets] in this crowded world to which so enormously destructive a weapon as the atomic bomb can ever be counted as proportionate". But, he suggests, we must beware of confusing the "preliminary *conditions* which are required to justify the very undertaking of a war of self-defence, and the *rules* which govern the conduct of a war justly undertaken". The use of nuclear weapons—at any rate on all but an insignificant minority of foreseeable occasions—would be a grave breach of these rules for the conduct of a just war; but "the cause itself does not become unlawful for those members of the self-defending State who limit themselves to morally lawful acts, or even necessarily for the State itself"—so long as the preliminary conditions of a just war remain satisfied. The distinction to which the eminent canonist here draws attention is a valid and important one. If this were not so, one would never be justified morally in embarking on a course of action which might at some stage result in unforeseen and unintended evil of any kind. But Dr. McReavy's application of the principle in this instance is extraordinary. For, on the one hand, he does not acknowledge that this distinction between "conditions" and "rules" must lose all significance where violations of those "rules"—far from being incidental aberrations—form a deliberate, systematic and indeed indispensable element in the whole undertaking. On the other hand, he implies that we must, in our attempts morally to assess a course of action, bear in mind only the indubitably certain results which will flow from it; the uncertain, hypothetical concomitants not only may, but must be ignored. "It may be highly unlikely that they [the conditions required for a justifiable war of self-defence] will be fulfilled (especially if megaton H-bombs for which there are hardly any legitimate targets are used); but . . . it is not impossible". True; but to conclude on the strength of this marginal theoretical possibility that there is no moral duty, or even no moral right "to contract out in advance from any such war by conscientious objection" is to argue not altogether unlike a Catholic who might defend his manufacturing and marketing of contraceptives on the grounds that although it is not very likely, it is nevertheless possible that people will buy them in order to melt down the rubber and make it into balls for their children to play with. Certainty, as St. Thomas never tires to insist—following Aristotle in this, and setting the pattern for the theological tradition of Catholic Christendom—is not to be had in matters of morals "where everything is contingent and variable".[1] "It is the mark of the properly brought-up man that he seeks only as much certainty in the various fields of enquiry as the nature of the subject-matter permits. And no such certainty is to be had in a subject full of contingency and variability as there is in one where everything is necessary and invariable".[2]

To make our choices exclusively in view of their "certain" consequences and resolutely to exclude from our horizon their likely results—no matter how strong this likelihood—is at best moral blindness, at worst hypocritical self-excuse. We must, in trying to come to a decision, have in mind the sort of use which after all is the *raison d'être* of nuclear weapons; the sort of use for which these weapons, and they only, are fitted by their nature; and the sort of use, we should add, which we know only too well they are intended for. We should know this in our hearts even without the public evidence of such intention in defence policy. It is after all inconceivable that expenditure on such a scale should be undertaken, public conscience roused in the least degree, for stakes as low as bombing a "conveniently if improbably concentrated" enemy force, for use on occasions which no strategist would expect even the most blundering of enemies to provide. And, if this were not enough, we have the evidence of publicly declared defence policy. It is at the foundations of this *not* to

[1] *Commentary to Aristotle's "Ethics"*, Bk. II, lect. 2.
[2] *ibid.*, Bk. I, lect. 2.

restrict ourselves to scrupulously limited targets, but to "present to any potential attacker the prospect of virtual annihilation of his own country" (cf. above, p. 31). Is it possible, in the face of such declarations, to base one's moral thinking upon theatrical possibilities which they explicitly rule out?

We shall have to return to considering the morality of threatening, as distinct from performing, such acts with a view to deterring an enemy. All we need to make clear at this point is that when we speak of the use—actual or threatened use—of nuclear weapons, it is in terms of their wholesale, indiscriminate, "massive" use that we must think. Failure to do so is simply to fail to think within the realities of our situation. Persistence in such moral escapism may well mean moral disintegration.

2. THE MORALITY OF POSSESSING NUCLEAR WEAPONS

Any honest and realistic assessment of our situation, then, justifies us in concluding that the chief use which is likely to be made of the nuclear weapons now being manufactured, tested and stored is morally inadmissable. To any likely use we must simply say "no". But what about having nuclear weapons, in the hope of never having to use them?

There is, here, a preliminary moral problem which it is as well to discuss first. It concerns the relation of doing something to intending to do it. It is a general moral principle (already referred to in previous chapters) that if an action is morally wrong, it is wrong to intend to do it, even if one never gets the chance to carry out one's intention. If an action is wrong no matter what the circumstances, it is wrong to intend to do it in any, no matter how carefully limited and specified, circumstances. If exploding nuclear weapons is morally wrong in any circumstances, it is morally wrong to

intend exploding them in any, no matter how carefully circumscribed conditions (e.g. "only if the Russians have dropped
one first", "if we are driven to it as a last resort in self-
defence", etc.).

When we have decided that something is evil, we have
committed ourselves to not intending it as well as to refraining from doing it. This is one of the moral principles on which
discussion of both the questions to which this section is devoted hinges.

Confusion on this question is so common that it is worth
subjecting this moral principle to logical dissection. Someone
may dispute the principle by saying "But I do not *really* intend to do X; I only intend to do it if Y". The moral plausibility of such a plea rests on its ambiguity; we may clarify
it in either of two ways:

(*a*) "If Y, I intend to do X"; i.e. my intention can be
described as "to do X", simply, without any conditions
attached; Y's being or not being the case is a condition under
which I form my intention to do whatever I intend to do, in
this case X; it does not enter my intention as the condition
of my doing X. Alternatively,

(*b*) "I intend to do X if Y"; i.e. my intention is to do X
if something is the case and not otherwise, i.e., under certain
conditions; Y's being or not being the case is part of my intention as the condition of my *doing* or not *doing* X; it is not the
condition of my forming the intention to do whatever I intend.

Now (*b*) is morally unambiguous. If X is absolutely wrong
under any circumstances, it is wrong to intend it whatever
is the case. If we substitute for X "dropping H-bombs" and
for Y "the Russians drop one first" or something of that kind,
it is obvious that since no such condition can render the *dropping* of H-bombs morally justifiable, no such condition can

render the *intention* to do so morally justifiable either. The plea interpreted in sense *(b)* must, therefore, clearly be rejected. It does, however, receive a certain appearance of moral plausibility from the fact that it can easily be confused with the sense *(a)*. If taken thus, it means, in effect, something like this: "I do not, at the moment, intend anything at all; I am waiting for the circumstances to arise in which I can form an intention; so long as Y is not the case (so long as the conditions in which I would *consider* dropping an H-bomb do not exist), the question of my intending to do or not to do X (to drop H-bombs or not) does not arise. I am therefore content not to make any decision at present, but simply to carry on and wait."

Such a suspension of decision may very easily become a cloak for refusing to face vital issues, or even for making decisions about them covertly, without explicitly and honestly facing the fact that one has in fact made them. At the very least, it lends colour to the moral confusion brought about by having decided that a certain course of actions (e.g. dropping H-bombs) is morally indefensible, and then refusing to face the consequences of such a decision during the interim period before the conditions of its execution are realized. Such confusion makes it desperately easy to act, in the present, as if no decision had been made while claiming, at the same time, that one has already rejected the morally repugnant course of action. We shall later on encounter good reasons against authentic and honest suspension of decision until the need is upon us; for the present we must simply be on our guard against pretending that we have decided when we are not in fact willing to accept the consequences of our decision.

If, then, we find that "having" nuclear weapons involves intending to explode them over predominantly civilian targets, no more need be said; this intention is criminal, just as the action is criminal. What we must examine is whether we are necessarily, in possessing such weapons, committed to such an intention.

It is sometimes said that possession of weapons capable of such appalling destruction as nuclear weapons is itself our best insurance against the risk of their being used. Knowledge by the enemy that retaliation in kind will follow any recourse to nuclear weapons, or possibly any major warlike aggression, will deter him from provoking such action. Each side will thus hold its nuclear weapons in permanent reserve, so to speak, and, with any luck, neither side will actually explode them, or even be driven to initiating war. We may therefore, it is concluded, legitimately carry on manufacturing and stockpiling nuclear weapons for this purpose, and under the protection of this "umbrella" work for disarmament and peace.

This is an argument of some force. But it is necessary to face the fact that it is based on a hope which it is difficult to maintain. It may be true that, so long as rational counsels prevail, fear alone may suffice to prevent both sides from being the first to cast their stones. But it is too much to assume that rational counsels will prevail. The world provides all the opportunities for a "failure of nerve": an official or an individual failure of nerve. The tensions may well become near-intolerable; the temptation to put an end to them, to grasp what presents itself as a golden opportunity, may well sway official policies, and hysteria—and possibly even technical errors in interpreting radar-information—may easily bring about individual actions not countenanced by existing policies. The risks are incalculable. One cannot safely give a child a bottle of arsenic. He may or may not swallow it—it is a gamble.

It is a gamble, and many of us would assess the risk of loss at so appalling a price that nothing could justify it. Others, those who urge this policy, may reply that if it is a gamble, they are prepared to stake all in the game. Success, they will say, offers the only chance of escape. Is it not worth taking the enormous risks, in the hope of averting disaster? But is such a gamble—whatever may be said about the ethics of gambling in general—morally justifiable? We must scrutinize this argument more closely.

"Having an H-bomb is not evil even though exploding it over enemy cities is". This is the premiss from which the argument starts, from which it goes on to say that if by (morally allowable) "having" there is so much as a chance of preventing its use, then let us go on to make and stock-pile H-bombs. We must examine the notion of "having an H-bomb" more closely at this point. It is clear that there are many things, among them many dangerous things, capable of criminal use, which a man may quite blamelessly "have". I may have a gun, without thereby being guilty of the murder that I or someone else can commit with it. There is no reason, then, why I should not possess a gun, or should do my utmost to prevent someone else, not suspected of homicidal tendencies, from having one. If its possessor suddenly goes mad and shoots my worst enemy, I may even reap some benefit from his action, without having incurred any guilt; though, of course, if I am nearby I ought to try to stop him, and would be gravely guilty if I made no attempt to prevent him using it in this way.

Having an H-bomb, however, differs from having, for instance a gun, a television set, a car, a horsewhip, or a tin of rat-poison in two important respects. It differs in respect of the nature of the object possessed, as well as in the nature of the "possession" of the object. Let us take these separately and begin with the first of these differences. It does not make sense to say "guns are evil"; we can only speak of particular ways of using guns (e.g. to kill innocent people) as evil. Now the same may be said about H-bombs; but there is an important difference which makes it much more plausible to say that "H-bombs are evil". The difference is due to the fact that the use of H-bombs—if we discount the totally unreal, hypothetical case of use on isolated targets like ships at sea for which nobody would dream of manufacturing H-bombs—is always evil. They have only one use, and that is large-scale indiscriminate destruction. Having an H-bomb with the intention of using it in certain (specified or unspecified) circumstances is therefore necessarily evil, for it has been shown that *in any actual circumstances we can envisage,* the use of H-bombs is morally inadmissable. This is why the shorthand phrase "The H-bomb is evil" is plausible whereas "guns are evil" is not. If doing something is evil, intending to do it is equally evil. If dropping an H-bomb over Moscow is evil, intending to drop it ("if they drop one over London first", "as a last resort in our defence", etc.) is evil.

Does this mean that in "having" an H-bomb one is necessarily proclaiming an intention of using it? May it not be that the Minister of Defence, the Chiefs of Staff, etc., are not really intending to use the H-bomb when it comes to the point, but are really bluffing? And if this is the case, or if I am entitled to think that this is the case, am I not justified in standing by and acquiescing in their bluff, because, after all, it may have the desired result? The answer to this question brings us to the second respect in which "having" an H-bomb differs from "having" things like guns, etc., i.e. the difference in the kind of possession that is involved.

If ownership of an H-bomb were a simple matter like the ownership, say, of a gun, it would be plausible to argue that one is not under an obligation to stop someone else having a gun, even though one may suspect that he will not use it wisely. If his possessing the gun may bring about a highly desirable state of affairs, say deter a would-be murderer from getting in first, there may be much to be said in favour of even a doubtfully reliable man being allowed to have his gun.

But the analogy with the man having a gun breaks down: H-bombs are not things one man has and another has not, they are part of a nation's means of defence (at the best; at the worst, of aggression). In a democracy with representative government there is no ground for such a distinction between an owner of the weapon and an uncommitted spectator. If we have voted for people whom we know to support a policy of nuclear deterrence, we have decided to develop and manufacture these weapons, and even if it is a decision taken on our behalf rather than by ourselves, it is a decision and not something that has happened to us, and we may not escape our share of the responsibility for it. Further, we should consider very carefully whether, in our circumstances, and supposing all candidates to be committed to a wicked policy, merely not voting is enough. We may not shelter behind the collective "we" to shift the responsibility on to those of a "really responsible" inner circle. We cannot altogether disown responsibility for "their" decisions without pretending that we are spectators of a puppet-show when in fact our rôle approximates to that of the men who pull the strings.

For better or for worse, nuclear weapons are *ours* in a very strict sense, and *we* must decide on what to do with them. We may not argue thus: "The Minister of Defence (or Service Chiefs, etc.) when threatening to use nuclear weapons is either *(a)* intending to carry out his threat, or *(b)* bluffing and not intending to do so. If *(a)*, he is intending to do a crime and somebody ought to stop him; if *(b)*, he is not, and there is no obligation on me to expose his bluff, thereby preventing it from being, possibly, highly fruitful. We may not argue thus for the simple reason that the neat distinction between an "I" who looks on and a "they" who have nuclear weapons and decide about their use is unreal. If *(a)* the threat involved in possessing nuclear weapons for deterrence embodies a real intention to carry it out, I am a party to this—criminal—intention. If *(b)* the threat is not backed by the intention to carry it out, I am not helping someone else's—very profitable—deception to remain effective by conniving at it; I am deceiving myself along with my fellow-citizens. I am trying to have it both ways and thereby deceiving myself morally: I am disowning responsibility for a public decision, a decision taken on my behalf. In failing to say a clear "no" to this public commitment, and in failing to do all I can to get this "no" officially and publicly endorsed, I am doing one of two things: I am either admitting that I am identifying myself with the intention to use nuclear weapons in certain circumstances (specified or not) and prepared to back it when the time comes; or, if I refuse to acknowledge such an intention, I am seeking a way of escaping responsibility by taking refuge in the plea that such a decision is not "mine" but a community's. But there is no escape this way. Where vital moral issues such as this are in question, in the line of policy pursued by a nation, the individual *cannot* automatically claim to remain uncommitted; he must consider whether his silence is not an endorsement of the official policy, and whether in the absence of a clear protest he can evade responsibility for it. He may acquiesce in the policy of deterrence only at the cost of associating himself with the intention to carry out the threat in due course. Deterrence rests, in the end, on the intention to use nuclear weapons. It cannot but be morally repugnant for the same ultimate reason as is the use of the weapon held in reserve.

3. PRACTICAL CONSEQUENCES

Few of us are likely to be called upon to press the trigger of the mechanism to release a nuclear bomb, or even to pilot the aircraft which is to deliver it to its target. Is it enough for us to say "Yes, I recognize that this is a thing no man may do; but so far, at any rate, I have not been called upon to do this thing. If and when I am called upon to drop an H-bomb, I see that I must refuse to do so, even though the consequence of disobeying orders may be to face death by shooting. But for the present. . . "?

(i) *In the event of war*

Let us leave for the moment the various ways in which the last sentence may be finished, and look at the claim that refusing to perform the physical action of "dropping an H-bomb" is enough to keep a man's hands clean.

"Dropping an H-bomb" is not as simple an action as is, for instance, shooting a man with a rifle. It is not, in the same sense, *an* action. It involves a number of actions by several individuals—the crew of the aircraft to which the task is assigned, at least. And if it includes the pilot, the navigator, and so on, can we exclude the men who load the aircraft, the men who guide it from its take-off towards its target, and so on? It is unnecessary to trace the steps by which the circles of responsibility widen. Modern war is socially a complex phenomenon. Too many administrative decisions and too many phases of their execution are involved for it to be possible for any one involved in its machinery to claim that he is only doing "his bit", "let the other chaps look to what they are doing". Genuine ignorance of the total effect to which a man's individual action is a contribution may excuse obedience. But when I am knowingly taking part in organized evil-doing, I cannot plead that the blame is to be attached to the last link in the chain. In joining the gang, I have given it my support, I have associated myself with it in its aim, I have acknowledged that I intend what it intends to accomplish.

But this is still an over-simplification. It represents the R.A.F., or perhaps the armed forces as a whole, as a "gang" organized to deliver H-bombs and explode them over the enemy. This, at present, though perilously near the truth, is not true. For the R.A.F., and the armed forces in general, have other functions. The moral admissibility of some of these is open to question, but at any rate, we have not discussed those further problems here. Let us concede, for the sake of argument, that some of them are legitimate. There is, then, no reason why I should not enrol, say, in the R.A.F. in order to help in the defence of my country by pursuing the legitimate part which it exists to discharge in defence. Having done so, I may be taken by surprise one night when I am told to load an H-bomb on to a plane, or to drop it over Moscow. If I am told what it is that I am ordered to take part in, my choice is clear: I must say "No", and I can at least plead that I didn't know that this was part of the game, part of what might be asked of me. More likely, except for the small handful of those most directly concerned, I shall not know what I am taking part in until the task has been completed. Can I plead "not guilty" on the grounds that this was not what I joined the gang for, that "I did it unknowingly"?

Yes, on one condition: that there has been a clear, public declaration that my country will not, under any circumstances, use the H-bomb. In that case I may plead that I joined in good faith. On the other hand I do not need a public declaration to the effect that "we shall take the first opportunity to drop an H-bomb" to make it impossible for me to associate myself with any group that may be involved. I know only too well that there is a good supply of H-bombs; I know only too well that not only has their use not been utterly renounced, but that the defence policy which I am a party to carrying out is based on the readiness to use it—to use it, maybe, as a last resort, but to use it. Personal responsibility in modern war cannot be limited by refraining to take part in what are known to be morally repugnant courses of action, as and when they arise. It is quite unrealistic to think that there will be time to decide when the occasion arises, that "all will work out alright on the night". The machinery of modern war is too much dependent on long-term decisions about policy and strategy, about the weapons to be put into the hands of Service Chiefs, and on administrative and policy decisions of a long-term nature. The shape of war depends on the shaping done in peace; and the opportunities for individuals to alter its shape by their decisions are likely to be even fewer when war is being waged than they are in peace time. In modern warfare, responsibility must be accepted for all that is not antecedently, clearly and publicly ruled out, by any one who in any way participates in its waging.

This brings us to a second difficulty, one which we shall merely touch on. If it is clear that one may not participate in waging a war in which there is any chance or likelihood of using weapons known to exist whose use is morally inadmissible, what is meant by "participating in waging a war"? We have already encountered the difficulty of drawing a line between combatants and non-combatants when we were trying to discover the moral justification for the use of weapons capable of large-scale though not indiscriminate killing. We saw then that any weapon which obliterates this distinction, the use of which involves large-scale killing of non-combatants, is inadmissible as a means of warfare. Its use would be mass-murder. We are now faced with this same question in reverse: how can we draw the line between combatants and non-combatants in our own camp? How can we extricate ourselves from the mass of those engaged in mass-murder? The answer to this question is not completely clear. The reason for this is the same as the reason for the difficulty of drawing a precise line between combatant and non-combatant earlier: it lies in the complex nature of a society geared to total war, in which different members are involved in warfare to varying degrees and with varying directness. Some minimum conditions can, however, be stated without hesitation.

First, it is clearly impossible to enrol or to consent to conscription into any of the armed forces. These are of their nature geared to warfare. Their whole *raison d'être*, once war is being waged, is to be the wagers of war. Willingness to belong to them is equivalent to endorsing the waging of war. Equally clearly, we may rule out direct participation in the manufacture of armaments. One cannot engage in activities such as these without *thereby* declaring one's intention of participating in the war being waged. But once we go beyond these manifest ways of participating in warfare, it is difficult to say what it is legitimate to do in a society geared, as a whole, to waging war. Clearly, one who finds the means of waging war morally repugnant (or who finds a war waged without renunciation of the morally repugnant means repugnant), must, *at least,* dissociate his intention from the intention to wage the immoral war. Even the farm-labourer behind whose willingness to carry on with his job is concealed a willingness "to do his bit in the war", is morally, compromised. He is a party to the crime being committed.

It is important to distinguish the definition of *moral guilt and innocence,* under war conditions, from the related definition of *combatants and non-combatants.* The two pairs of terms tend to overlap; nevertheless, they remain distinct. A morally guilty man (for instance, an invalid wholly in sympathy with his country's immoral conduct) may be a non-combatant; whilst a morally innocent man (such as a soldier, whose conscience—though objectively misinformed—is in a state of "good faith") may be a highly destructive fighter. It is the degree of their strategic involvement that finally determines the status of individuals as potential military targets. Moral guilt, however, may be incurred either by actually consenting to be a combatant in circumstances recognized as evil (and to this extent the problem of avoiding guilt is identical with that of defining, and avoiding, "combatant" action), or it may be incurred simply by an *interior* participation or consent, conflicting with one's moral judgement of the situation. Even a job of little or no strategic importance could thus occasion grave moral guilt, if the intention is to identify oneself with the war as a whole.

But how far ought the dissociation of one's intention from the intention of waging war to be publicly displayed in the choice of action? I can see no clear-cut answer to this question. Perhaps, in the end, working for the succour and relief of suffering offers the most obvious alternative; perhaps, for many, continuation in their chosen calling or facing imprisonment as the penalty for refusing to be absorbed into the war-machine may commend itself as the more effective witness to the truth.

(ii) At the present time

So much for the questions concerned with the stand a man is to make in a society at war, when he has seen that the means of waging it to which it is committed are to be morally rejected without condition. But—at the time of writing—we are not at war, and we are faced with the problem of how to make our witness relevant and, if possible, effective within a society preparing for a war it hopes to avoid.

If the questions which we have been discussing, questions about nuclear weapons, their use in war, our country's reliance upon them as an essential part of its strategy of defence and of its foreign policy, are the vital moral issues of our day, what line of action is open to the ordinary citizen who has come to reach a moral decision on these problems? For those who are unable to see any *moral* objection—and hence overriding objection—to a recourse to weapons like the H-bomb, the answer will be relatively simple. They may acquiesce, perhaps with a heavy heart, in the current policies. Alternatively, they may criticize them or even reject them on other grounds, on the grounds of their ineffectiveness, dangers, expense, or inexpediency of whatever kind. But what about those who have come to see that they must simply say "no" unconditionally to the use of such weapons and therefore to all policies based on the threat of their use in the appropriate circumstances?

In the first place, this certainly means *refusal of military service*. Since "deterrence" at least implies an *ultimate* reliance on immoral methods, and "joining the gang"—in whatever capacity—gives knowing support to this immoral war machine, personal responsibility cannot be evaded by getting "into some branch of service which has nothing to with mass-destruction-weapons".[1] As has been shown in the previous

[1] Canon F. H. Drinkwater's "Jude", in his "Conversation on the Hydrogen Bomb", *Morals and Missiles*, p. 43. "No, it's a man's duty to answer the call to defend his country. That's part of the Fourth Commandment. But I think he should try to get into some branch of service which has nothing to do with mass-destruction-weapons. And if he is ordered to use such weapons in war, or train for them in peace-time, I think he should say : No, this is where I have to disobey orders, this is where I must obey God rather than man. After all, that has always been the duty of a Christian when ordered to do things that outrage humanity. We've been getting our consciences

section, in the circumstances of modern war, "responsibility must be accepted for all that is not antecedently, clearly and publicly ruled out, by anyone who in any way participates in its waging". Similarly, military service *at this moment* implies an endorsement of the policy, at this moment, of "massive nuclear bombardment" and "virtual annihilation".

Apart from making one's own personal stand in refusing to participate in any way in carrying out any phase of these policies, it is difficult to see what line of action is open. Clearly such a moral rejection of nuclear warfare is equivalent to renouncing any intention to have or to use such weapons, under any circumstances, no matter what others do, that is to say, it commits us to *unconditional renunciation of these weapons*.

It involves more than this, however: if we regard an act as criminal, we cannot wish that someone else should do it even if we stand to profit by their crime. We should therefore have to renounce all treaties and alliances based on a policy which has not renounced nuclear warfare. We are not, of course, responsible for American policy as we are for British; we can only wish that Americans—and everybody else, for that matter—renounce the evil. What we may not do is to *want* others to perpetrate the crime we have renounced, still less may we be partners in any arrangement binding others to perpetrate it for our benefit. Thus, so far as the United States are concerned, we must hope that they, as well

a bit blunted lately, but it's time to make a stand again and distinguish right from wrong even in war." As Canon Drinkwater has himself voiced similar conclusions elsewhere, we may take it that he agrees with Jude. Our disagreement with Canon Drinkwater, on this point, does not spring from any disagreement *in principle* about the rights and duties of defence, but from a difference about the implications of military service in present circumstances. We should like to pay tribute to Canon Drinkwater's patient, and often lonely, advocacy of the case against indiscriminate warfare.

as Britain, will discard nuclear weapons; and, so far as Britain is concerned, demand that there will also be a *withdrawal from N.A.T.O.*—for N.A.T.O. is based on precisely this sort of commitment, and indeed involves the provision of bases from which "massive retaliation" can be launched.

These are political consequences of a moral decision, and political action is required to bring them about. It seems inescapable, once the moral case against nuclear warfare is seen for what it is, that it would be seen as of an urgency such as warrants the subordination of all other political obligations to the attempt to make one's moral stand politically effective. Whenever there are international negotiations for *multilateral disarmament*, we should indicate our support, encouraging our representatives to throw caution to the winds, and—without pretending to a security that is beyond us—accept those measures of disarmament to which we are, anyway, committed in conscience. Mr. Khrushchev has offered complete mutual disarmament. There is no excuse for not taking him at his word. For *we* are in any case committed to abandoning these weapons, on which our military defence is now dependent. We are committed to *unilateral action*; and if Russia is prepared for "controlled" disarmament, that is a bonus we must welcome with gratitude.

Indeed, since we are thus obliged to renounce nuclear weapons, irrespective of what the other side may do, and since without these weapons we could not, in the last resort, be militarily successful, Western governments should be pressed to face up to the problem of *non-violent resistance*. It is no good underestimating the challenge of this problem. But it is no good, either, disowning the moral compulsions towards non-violence in our time.

Apart from making use of whatever means we have for propagating these conclusions, there is at least one line of

simple political action open to us : might it not be obligatory
in conscience to vote only for such a candidate who is prepared to endorse our unconditional rejection of nuclear warfare and to face the implications of this rejection? This may
outrage one's political allegiance; but it is a feature of our
time that some of the deepest and most genuine political issues
cut across the existing party-divisions. This is certainly one
such issue; for here, in a double sense, our very humanity is
at stake.

To try to "keep one's hands clean" may be simple
Pharisaism. In this case it is simply a refusal to capitulate to
the forces that have gone so far to undermine our humaneness
that we still speak the language of morals while consenting
to exempt warfare from the realm of morality. We are being,
increasingly, swept along the current towards accepting war
as a master, with a dynamism of its own, to which our standards of right and wrong are not applicable, a process which
enslaves those who participate in it and subdues them to its
purposes, much in the same way as does a totalitarian state.
In reminding ourselves of moral limits we are reasserting that
all human activity stands under the law; and that if we are
not prepared to include war under this, then we must re-
pudiate it as a possible activity—that is, an activity about
which we can at least ask the question "is it right or is it
wrong"?

To a Christian, our common human situation presents its
special need for his faith and compassion. A Christian's insis-
tence must be, first of all, on accepting the demands of our
common humanity. He will have added reasons for doing so :
in a world in which they are threatened, as they are on so
many sides today, this must become part of his witness to
Christ. This witness would be decisively mutilated in the absence of a stand against the "sustained contemporary on-

slaught", not only upon human mercy, but even on the acknowledgement of common human standards as binding upon conduct. It is perhaps through his unconditional submission to such standards that the individual Christian can best fulfil his part in the Church's mission: to show forth perpetually in the world something of God's justice and unfathomable love for men. He may pray for the assistance of the Church as a whole to render such a witness more effective; but it is better that Christians should speak, even if stammeringly and lacking a single voice, than to disown their vocation to transform the world into new life in Christ by the power of faith and love.

IV
CONSCIENCE IN COMMISSION

P. T. Geach

IN THIS chapter I shall be concerned not so much with the substantive question, of the rightness of using nuclear weapons, as with reasons that have been alleged why individuals should not trouble their consciences about this question at all. For one thing, it has been seriously argued that since as yet we have not to make any actual decision, we ought not to trouble ourselves; that the only logical course "is to reserve one's final judgement of the possible issues until (which God forbid!) they become actual".[1] This argument cannot be lightly dismissed. Even as a matter of ordinary human prudence, there is much to be said for not crossing bridges till you come to them. And spiritual writers warn us that the devil often suggests to us the question what we ought to do in circumstances that have not arisen and may never arise, and tries to hurry us into a wrong hypothetical decision; he thus may have all the satisfaction of leading us to form a mortally sinful intention, without any of the trouble of contriving circumstances in which an actual decision would be unavoidable; and we ought to foil his malice and cunning by giving no other answer to the question he presses upon us than, "I will do as the Lord wills", and by trusting in God that in an actual case we shall be given grace to decide rightly.

[1] Dr. L. L. McReavy, "The Debate on the Morality of Future War", *Clergy Review*, February 1960.

We cannot, however, avoid the necessity of present decision as to whether a given nuclear-war policy is right. If a policy is one that it would be wicked to execute, then it is also wicked to counsel it and wicked to make plans for executing it. It is a present question of conscience whether an elector may vote for a parliamentary candidate whom he knows to be strongly in favour of a certain policy; whether an officer in the armed forces may instruct men in a technique of destroying cities; whether a labourer may work on a rocket site. These questions, however we decide them, have to be decided now; yet their answers are inescapably connected with the answers to hypothetical questions about the actual use of nuclear arms in war.

We may, however, on various grounds, be urged to put our consciences *in commission* about these matters. It has often happened in history that someone in high authority, like a king or archbishop, has felt unable to take some decisive action in person; instead, he has temporarily delegated his powers to a commission. He may have suspected, or even known, that the commissioners would do on his behalf something that he would have thought it very wrong for himself to do; he could nevertheless feel that he was quit of his burden of decision and had shifted it off onto other men's shoulders. I shall here try to review these grounds for evading a personal exercise of conscience—in what sems to me a descending order of merit.

1. CONSCIENCE AND THE CHURCH

We are of course bound, as Dr. McReavy insists, to inform our consciences by the *magisterium* of the Church (p. 80); and in this connexion we must carefully study, as in the following chapter, the relevant papal utterances. The late Pope unequivocally asserted the right of self-defence and the duty of citizens to take part in carrying out their govern-

ments' lawful defence policies; he also, while not condemning
the use of any *kind* of weapon unconditionally, unequivocally
denounced the use of weapons for wholesale indiscriminate
destruction. In essence, this was a reassertion of traditional
principles about warfare, as applicable even in the modern
world. How these principles should be applied is another matter. Disputants may argue that in the actual situation the
Pope *must* have intended a direct application of his utterances
in support—or in condemnation—of actual Western policies.
This manner of arguing can be used by both sides, and must
surely be inconclusive. It is surely the most prudent view that
the Holy See has reaffirmed certain traditional principles,
whose application is still a task for our own consciences.

We are in any case not to expect a direct and particular
guidance from the Holy See on all matters of grave moral
import. Even man's natural reason is not so weak and corrupted that he can *never* tell right from wrong with certainty
apart from revelation and the *magisterium* of the Church—particularly as regards sins whose deformity is very great. A
Catholic who helped in Himmler's extermination policies
could hardly excuse himself by the plea that he had never
learned of any specific condemnation of those policies by the
Holy See.

Failing such direct and particular guidance, we may be
counselled to follow the guidance of the local hierarchy and
ask no further questions for conscience' sake. But one's own
diocesan may be most uncertain as to the right policy. Moreover, the loving trust that an individual may feel in his own
diocesan ought not to prevent him from realizing that a
general principle of following one's own diocesan in matters
of conscience is an unsafe one, which would often have led
people wrong in the past. The English hierarchy supported
the criminal ambition of Henry V; and with the exception of

one holy martyr, they supported the impious claims of Henry VIII. These are extreme cases, but it is just such cases that show whether a suggested general rule can *always* be followed in an emergency.

Again, we are sometimes counselled to find some theologian and pin our conscience to his coat. Denzinger is full of theological opinions calculated to justify the wicked ways of the world and condemned by the Holy See only after they had long been freely taught. I cannot, however, here enter on the vexed question of probabilism. But it is an accepted teaching that a good person may "by connaturality", by being that sort of person, be better informed as to the particular exercise of a virtue than a theologian who is learned in moral theology. The brave mother who recently carried an ectopically conceived child to full term did better than if she had followed a theological opinion that she could have the child removed before it was viable. In any event, it is one thing for a man to follow a theological opinion in good faith, even if the opinion is later papally condemned; it is quite another thing to decide on a wicked policy and then quiet one's conscience by finding a theologian who will defend it. Ignorance of the divine law produced in that way is affected ignorance, which does not remove or mitigate the guilt of an objectively wicked action, but aggravates it. Let us remember our Lord's words about blind leaders of the blind. By our Lord's own testimony, the authority of the scribes and Pharisees was not usurped but lawful; they sat in the seat of Moses; but not all of their opinions could lawfully be followed.

2.   CONSCIENCE AND THE STATE

So far I have considered suggestions that we should leave the decision in these grave matters to some lawful spiritual authority. It is quite a different thing if we are asked to put our conscience in the pocket of the State. It is sometimes supposed that a Christian citizen must presume that what his rulers do in his defence is right—a presumption only to be overruled in very grave circumstances—because the ordinary man must necessarily be ignorant of the factors that determine a government's decision. It may well be argued against this that the dangers of a nuclear war of themselves constitute a consideration grave enough to suspend such a presumption in favour of the government. But such an argument is unnecessary for my purposes, if I can show that no such general presumption now exists.

My argument rests at this point upon facts of great notoriety, which are yet so much the framework of our lives that they are easily overlooked. It is only since the Reformation that Christian States—I use this phrase as a convenient short designation for States whose citizens are for the most part validly baptized and nominally Christian—have claimed an unrestricted autonomous right of legislation. This claim was a natural result of the Reformation. First of all, it was held that *cuius regio, eius religio*—subjects must follow their princes in religion, and even, as in England, in changes of religion; nowadays the State sits an impartial arbiter between various forms of Christianity and infidelity, and, like Gallio, cares for none of these things.

Such claims would have appeared monstrous to any medieval thinkers who would now be recognized to have expressed the mind of the Church. For them, a Christian State was *de jure* no autonomous authority; it was only a part of "the whole corps of Christendom", the *respublica Christiana*, whose supreme head on earth is the Vicar of Christ. Laws made by a particular Christian State were held *ipso facto* null and void if they ran counter to the metropolitan law of Christendom, just as laws made by a particular State of the

Union are if they contravene the federal law of the United States. No prescription could ever make such laws valid, for against the divine law and the authority of the Holy See there can be no prescription. For example, no Christian State could make a valid law making impediments to marriage not recognized by the Holy See, or removing diriment impediments, or making priests and religious liable to conscription and criminal prosecution. Such laws would on this view remain for ever null and void, however long a Christian State might succeed in enforcing them. No oath of office could bind anybody to enforce such laws. And the *general claim* to make laws regardless of the metropolitan law of Christendom would not only be of no effect to validate such laws but would be an act of open rebellion against the *respublica Christiana*; some would have held, with Aquinas, that such rebellion *ipso facto* deprived a ruler of his claim on his subjects' allegiance; at any rate, such a ruler could then be deposed by judicial sentence of the Holy See.

It may well be said that the traditional theology of allegiance, which I have here sketched, was always open to doubt, and is anyhow now inapplicable. But I cannot see any sound principle for discriminating between the traditional theology of allegiance and the traditional doctrine of the just war. On both matters our theology derives from what Dr. McReavy (p. 80) calls "the golden age of Christian theology"; and it would be hard to produce any papal document on either matter to show that the old teaching is now officially abandoned.

As regards the modern application of these principles, I have no competence to suggest how an up-to-date theory of allegiance would look. I would, however, suggest that we cannot be confident that by reason of a long past apostasy States have reverted to the juridical independence that heathen rulers have under the law of nature. In merely civil affairs, long past usurpation or rebellion, however unjust, may be the ground of an indubitable present right; but if baptized persons seek to throw off the easy yoke of Christ, they may well find that, in Hobbes's words, they can shake off their ease, but not their yoke. As regards individuals, this is certainly still the mind of the Church; a Catholic cannot put himself in the position of a Protestant or pagan as regards the Church's marriage laws because he apostatized years before the projected marriage. And if the Church, for reasons of prudence, does not assert her rights against rebellious Christian States, that does not show that such rights are non-existent.

The only positive conclusion I do want to draw is that Christian subjects of a Christian State cannot safely put their consciences in commission by acting on the presumption that what the State does is right. If the many standing legislative claims of a modern State are of such a character that grave doctors of a former time would have held they forfeited entirely the State's right to command its subjects' obedience, then I do not see how this presumption in favour of the State has any particular weight.

We should further remember that countries behind the Iron Curtain—Russia, Poland, Hungary, Bohemia, Prussia—are, equally with the Western nations, parts of divided and apostate Christendom. God alone knows his elect; but millions of Christians practise their religion in those countries, where it costs more to do so. Let us lay to heart the rebuke of the prophet when unfaithful Israel was about to press ruthlessly home a military advantage over unfaithful Juda (2 Paralip, 28); the Israelites repented in time to avert God's anger.

3. CONSCIENCE THREATENED?

The last two arguments that I have to consider are arguments *ad horrendum*. In each of them, some evil is presented as so utterly unbearable that we shall be driven to say to our governments: We fully authorize you to do *anything* on our behalf if only you can secure us against this intolerable evil —even if you can do it only by exposing millions of us to death and ruthlessly destroying the enemy. But the evils that are thus presented as intolerable differ in kind. One argument appeals to the danger of our being forced into mortal sin, say by brain-washing, if the communists should win a "conventional" war; the other appeals to our aversion to servitude under a hateful ruler.

Mortal sin is indeed the greatest of evils, and we must be prepared to suffer any other evils sooner than commit it. But the idea that the communists have invented some scientific technique by which they can interiorly convert our rebellious wills and make us love Big Brother is at once heretical, conceptually confused, and factually ill-founded. It is heretical to deny that God gives every man sufficient grace to avoid mortal sin; and the heresy becomes ludicrous if people suppose that laboratory investigations can circumvent the workings of God's grace. Again, no one can sin mortally except by his own free will; and it is a contradiction in terms to suppose that some scientific technique could guarantee what a man did of his own free will; e.g. the words he uttered would then *both* proceed from his own choice *and* independently of his choice, be guaranteed by some circumstances arranged by his captors. Of course his captors may have mastered some technique that will ensure that words expressing blasphemy and apostasy come out of a man's mouth; but if they use such a technique, they have *ipso facto* ensured that the utterance of such words is not a human act at all, let alone a mortal sin. The knowledge that one's personality had been so violated might tempt one to despair, as an act of rape might tempt a woman; but this is a temptation that can be prepared against and resisted.

"That is all very well in theory—you don't know what these brain-washes can do in practice!" Well, we know they do not always succeed; not with Turks taken prisoner in Korea, nor with Jehovah's Witnesses; and, as St. Thomas More says, "is it not then more than shame that Christ shall see his Catholics forsake his faith rather than suffer the same for heaven and very glory?"[1] If Turks could resist brain-washing out of patriotism, and Jehovah's Witnesses out of the hatred and pride of their heresy, can we fear that Christ will desert the faithful? For faith is not, as some novels represent it, an arbitrary gift of God, something like an ear for music, which he may take away for no fault of one's own; and no new technique can snatch the elect from their Saviour's hand.

To be sure, subjection to the communists would greatly increase temptations to apostasy. But this does not justify us in abdicating moral responsibility to a government, in order to be sure that we shall not thus be tempted. What right have we to expect immunity from severe temptation? It might as well be argued that, to escape a risk of grave temptation, a man may personally commit suicide or murder.

The fear of servitude is a much baser fear. For though Father Paul Crane speaks of political freedom as a "spiritual good", and thinks that the choice to defend it when defence is known to be hopeless may be justified by "the primacy of the

[1] *Utopia,* and *Dialogue of Comfort against Tribulation,* Everyman's Library, p. 417.

spiritual",[1] it is perfectly obvious that freedom, like wealth
and honourable standing and fair fame, is only one of the
goods of fortune, which God's good providence may give us or
deny. To make political freedom an absolute value is a pagan
Stoic attitude, not a Christian one; and a determination to
"defend" it "at all costs", even the lives of most people on
both sides, is much less justifiable than Cato's suicide.

Civil order and legal justice are values of the same rank as
political freedom; and one thing to weigh in the balance is
that in the aftermath of a nuclear war these values would
inevitably be sacrificed. It is difficult to be a devout practicing
Christian in Poland or Russia; it would not be easier in a state
of affairs where civil authority had totally broken down and
every man's life and goods were at the mercy of any armed
ruffian. Even real spiritual values could then be attained only
much more arduously; and as for the liberty in whose "defence" this state of affairs had been brought about—it would
be a wry jest to speak of it.

In these evil times we should seek comfort not from
"brilliant and penetrating essays", but from the writings of
the Saints; and I have found More's Dialogue particularly
comforting. If we read the beginning of the third book, we
can see that what Christians now fear of communist conquest is very much the same as what they then feared of
Turkish conquest.[2] And I shall end by quoting what he says
about the "spiritual value" of liberty and the fear of losing
it:[3]

Our froward mind maketh every good thing hard, and that to
our own more hurt and harm. But in this case, if we will be

[1] The Rev. Paul Crane, S.J., "Catholics and Nuclear War", *The
Month*, October 1959, p. 227.
[2] *Op. cit.*, pp. 310-312.
[3] *Ibid.*, p. 367.

good Christian men, we shall have great cause gladly to be content for the great comfort that we may take thereby, which we remember that in the patient and glad doing of our service unto that man for God's sake, according to his high commandment by the mouth of St. Paul, *servi obedite dominis carnalibus* (Eph. 6, 5), we shall have our thank and our whole reward of God.

Finally, if we remember the great humble meekness of our Saviour Christ himself, that he being very Almighty God *humiliavit semetipsum formam servi accipiens*, humbled himself and took the form of a bondman or a slave, rather than his Father should forsake us, we may think ourself *(sic)* very unkind caitiffs, and very frantic fools too, if, rather than to endure this worldly bondage for a while, we would forsake him that by his own death delivered us out of everlasting bondage of the devil, and will for our short bondage give us everlasting liberty.

V

THE WITNESS OF THE CHURCH

Roger Smith

1. THE "JUST WAR" TRADITION

Ecclesia abhorret a sanguine—the Church shrinks from bloodshed. This has been, and always will be, a watchword for all Christians, in all places, at all times. In the first two centuries after Christ, under persecution, there were few Christian soldiers, and even after the Edict of Milan in 313 A.D. Christians remained largely aloof from military service. The main reason for this was not, as is sometimes supposed, a reluctance to perform idolatrous immolations, since this was not generally required of soldiers under the rank of centurion,[1] but a general preference for the "weapons of light" as against the sword. There was, too, for those who did serve a distinction between *militare* (to do military service) and *bellare* (to wage war), a distinction perhaps between policing and preserving order within the *Orbis Romanus* and taking part in bloody wars with barbarian forces on the fringe of that "world". Nevertheless, there were few who questioned the lawful use of force in certain circumstances, though many re-

[1] Tertullian points out, in *De Idololatria XIX*, that there was no necessity for idolatrous immolations in the Militia Caligata (the Sandalled Army), that is among the ordinary ranks and officers under the rank of centurion. One of the fullest accounts on the early Church and military service may be found (apart from Vanderpol and Stratmann) in the article on "Militarisme" by Dom H. Leclerq in *Dictionnaire d'Archéologie Chrétienne et de Liturgie*. Vol. XI.

garded killing in warfare as an all too probable occasion of sin. This last realization undoubtedly prompted the severe penances imposed by ecclesiastical synods during the ninth, tenth and eleventh centuries A.D., upon those who had shed blood in battle.

St. Basil (d. 379), St. Athanasius (d. 373) and St. Ambrose (d. 397) conceded that killing in war for the sake of the common good, the protection of one's own soil and of religion could be justified. It was St. Augustine (d. 430) who appealed to the Emperor for defence against the Donatists, who were attacking Christians. It was Augustine who laid the foundations of the traditional teaching on the just war. On these foundations (incorporated in Gratian's Decretal 1148 A.D.) the teaching of St. Thomas Aquinas, Vittoria, Suarez and Bellarmine was built .

The idea of a "punitive" war, as envisaged by St. Thomas and St. Augustine, was not taken up by subsequent generations to the same extent as the concept of a defensive war— the defence of rights unjustly attacked. St. Thomas laid down three conditions for a just resort to arms; legitimate authority *(legitima auctoritas)*, just cause *(justa causa)*, and right intention *(recta intentio)*. To these was added, by Suarez (d. 1617) and Bellarmine (d. 1621), a fourth condition—the right way of conducting a war *(debitus modus)*. A fifth condition, that there must be moral certainty that the just cause will win, comes from Cajetan (d. 1534) and Vittoria (d. 1546). Cajetan wrote: "The ruler must be morally certain that the just cause will win. Therefore the state waging a just war must be stronger than its opponent, otherwise the war cannot achieve its purpose." A further condition is usually listed; that all other methods of righting the injustice done have failed.

The last three conditions add nothing to St. Thomas's three, except to show the fuller implications of the right intention, "that good may be furthered and evil avoided". Employing unjust means or undertaking a war without reasonable prospects of success would clearly indicate a wrong intention, as would any unnecessary recourse to war.

It was St. Alfonsus Liguori (d. 1797) who wrote, "War brings such evils with it—such harm to Religion and to the innocent—that in practice it is hardly ever justifiable.[1] This would not be a difficult thesis for an historian-cum-moral theologian to sustain, on the evidence available. It would require the application of principles to events which actually took place and an assessment of events against the stated aims and intentions of those who held the reins of authority.

Similarly, in examining the moral implications of any future major conflict between nations or groups of nations, it is necessary to consider the actual events of the last twenty years (a period well-documented and recorded) and the statements and actions of the responsible statesmen and military leaders of that era, but more particularly the declared policies and intentions for the future (made often enough by the same people or their close collaborators).

It is the purpose of this chapter to document some of the authoritative statements and teaching upon which such discussion must necessarily be based.

The traditional conditions which must all be fulfilled for a war to be deemed justifiable may be summarized as follows:

1. It must be declared by the lawful authority.
2. It must be undertaken for a grave and just cause proportionate to the evils brought about by its waging.

---

[1] cf. "Today, with the new total methods of waging war, if anyone asks whether there can still be a just war, we must answer, theoretically yes, but in practice, probably never." Mgr. Colli, Bishop of Parma, in an article in *L'Osservatore Romano* during 1949.

3. The whole prosecution of the war must be carried out with a right intention—"that good may be furthered and evil avoided".
4. The war must be rightly conducted, and restrained within the limits of justice and love.
5. There must be real probability of success.
6. It must be undertaken as a last resort after all other means have been unsuccessful.

2. THE CHURCH AND "MODERN WAR"

Leaving aside for the moment the particular development of nuclear weapons, how do the traditional conditions apply in general to the warfare of our age?

In 1922 Cardinal Faulhaber, during a sermon on the occasion of the Disarmament Conference pointed out:

> We live in a period of transition; and just as in other questions, so too, in the question of war and peace, a change of heart will be effected. . . . Even the teaching of moral theology in regard to war will speak a new language. It will remain true to its old principles, but in regard to the question of the permissibility of war, it will take account of the new facts. . . .

Many of these facts are alluded to in the following extracts from the late Pope Pius XII's encyclicals, Christmas and Easter messages given during the last war. It must be clear, that in any papal address or encyclical received and commented on by Christians and non-Christians the world over, every word will have been weighed and carefully chosen. The forthrightness and plain speaking of the following, is, therefore, the more remarkable.

> The unspeakable calamity of war, which Pius XI foresaw with deep misgiving . . . is now upon us as a tragic reality. . . . Since the world seems to have forgotten the peaceful message of Christ, the voice of reason and Christian brotherhood, we have

been forced to witness a series of acts irreconcilable alike with the precepts of positive international law and those of the law of nature, as well as with the elementary sentiments of humanity; acts which show in what a vicious circle the juridical sense becomes involved when it is led simply by considerations of expediency. Among such crimes we must include a calculated act of aggression against a small industrious and peaceful nation . . . atrocities (by whichever side committed) and the unlawful use of destructive weapons against non-combatants and refugees, against old men and women and children; a disregard for the dignity, liberty and life of man, showing itself in actions which cry to Heaven for vengeance.[1]

September 1943 brought further doubts as to whether the continuance of the war could be either reasonable or justifiable:

In every land, men's minds are being alienated from the cult of violence, as they see in the horrid harvest of death and destruction its deserved condemnation.
In all nations there grows an aversion to the brutality of the methods of total war, which tend to pass beyond every just limit and every norm of divine and human law.
More tormenting than ever, there comes to soften the minds and hearts of men the doubt whether the continuation of hostilities—and of such hostilities—is and can be said to be still in conformity with national interests, or reasonable and justifiable in the light of Christian and human conscience.[2]

The following passage from the Christmas Message of 1943 powerfully underlines this condemnation of total war:

Unfortunately the world, as it looks around, must still behold with horror the reality of strife and destruction. . . . We see,

[1] *In questo giorno*, Allocation to the Sacred College, 28 December 1939. *Acta Apostolicæ Sedis*, xxxii, Series II, Vol. vii, p. 7 ss.
[2] AAS—xxxv-II-x, p. 278.

indeed, only a conflict which degenerates into that form of warfare that excludes all restriction and restraint (total war), as if
it were the apocalyptic expression of a civilization in which ever-
growing technical progress is accompanied by an ever greater
decline in the realm of the soul and of morality. It is a form
of war which proceeds without intermission on its horrible way
and piles up slaughter of such a kind that the most blood-stained
and horrible pages of past history pale in comparison with it.
The peoples have had to witness a new and incalculable perfec-
tion of the means and arts of destruction while at the same
time they see an interior decadence which, starting from the
weakening and deviation of the moral sense, is hurtling ever
downward toward the state where every human sentiment is
being crushed and the light of reason is eclipsed, so that the
words of wisdom are fulfilled: "They were all bound together
with one chain of darkness". (Wisdom 13: 71).[1]

Apart from the raids on Hamburg, Cologne and Berlin in
1943, it was not until 1944 that the Allies adopted the policy
of "area" or "obliteration" bombing; this occasioned not only
the protests of the German hierarchy, but those of the hier-
archies of France and of Australia, the Cardinal Primate of
Belgium, as well as a number of individual Bishops.[2] The Pope,
in his Appeal for Prayer for Peace, in May 1944, declared:

> Wherever we turn our eyes and heart, this murderous and
> fratricidal war shows us nothing but sorrow, destruction, and
> immense ruin.[3]

A further statement, in his Christmas Message of 1944,
summed up:

> Meanwhile, one duty is binding upon all, and it brooks no
> delay, no postponement, no hesitation, no subterfuge: every-

[1] AAS xxxvi-II-xi, p. 12.
[2] See *The Tablet*, 20 May 1944.
[3] AAS xxxvi-II-xi.

thing possible must be done once and for all to ban and proscribe the war of aggression as a legitimate solution of international disputes or as an instrument for achieving national
aspirations. The past has seen many attempts made in this
direction. All have failed, and they will continue to fail until
such time as the sounder part of the human race assumes the
firm resolve, and maintains it with holy obstinacy as a duty of
conscience, to bring to completion the task which former gener
ations had inaugurated, but without sufficient seriousness or
resolution.
If there was ever a generation which must have heard the inner
bidding of conscience to "declare war upon war", it is certainly
the present . . . the theory of war as an apt and proportionate
means of solving international conflicts is now out of date.[1]

From the foregoing extracts it may be seen that at least two
of the conditions required for a justifiable war are in question: the second condition that the just cause must be proportionate to the evils brought about by the war; and the
fourth condition, that the war must be conducted within the
limits of justice and love.

In taking "account of the new facts", the position taken
up by Cardinal Ottaviani merits particular attention. In the
first volume of his *Institutiones Juris Publici Ecclesiastici* (writ-
ten some years before being created a Cardinal), under the
heading "War is to be altogether forbidden", he maintains of
war today:

The conditions which theoretically make it justifiable and per-
missible are never present. . . . Nowhere can there be a cause
in proportion to so much evil, slaughter and destruction and
such denial of religious and moral values.[2]

---

[1] AAS xxxvii-II-12, 6 18.
[2] *Institutiones Juris Publici Ecclesiastici* Vol. I. (*Jus Publicium Inter-
num, Pars 1, Titulus iii art 3. Relationes Societarum Perfectarum in Statu
Conflictus) Principium* 2—Vatican Polyglot 3rd Edn. 1947, pp. 149-55.

Among the many reasons he gives for taking this viewpoint, he mentions the deliberate slaughter of innocent non-combatants and the reprisals it provokes; the defiance of international laws that have been solemnly ratified and agreed upon among nations; the spread of crime and moral evil following the war; the ease with which wars spread to other nations; secret preparation of arms, which makes certainty of success a hazardous prophecy. Hence,

> Leaving aside the question of a defensive war (and even this under fixed conditions), fought in the defence of the state against actual and unjust attack by another state, there can no longer be a just war which a state may undertake to retrieve its rights.

These extracts accord very closely with the above-quoted sections from Pius XII's Christmas Messages of 1943 and 1944.

3. STATEMENTS ON NUCLEAR WARFARE

The protests against "area", "obliteration", or "saturation" bombing registered in 1944 by members of the hierarchy in various countries were made because this policy meant the deliberate destruction of non-combatants contrary to both moral and international law. The indiscriminate killing of over one hundred thousand Japanese in Hiroshima and Nagasaki in the following year was an inevitable fulfilment of such a policy.[1] These were not the wayward acts of bomber

---

[1] Dresden, which was raided by Allied aircraft (c. 3,150 bombers were used to mount three raids in thirty-six hours) in February 1945, was said to be full of German forces and housed several important war industries. In addition to its normal population of 600,000 the city was crammed with 300,000 to 500,000 refugees fleeing from the Russian advance. The communiqué from the Supreme Allied H.Q. describing the operation contained the following: "The Dresden raid was designed to cripple communications. The fact

crews acting without authority, nor could they possibly be described as examples of "double effect".

The discussions on the policy of air attack at the Casablanca Conference are recorded in *Army Air Forces in World War II*. References are made to attacks on "morale", "political objectives" (cities are specifically mentioned) and to the "progressive undermining of enemy morale and economic organization".

That these weapons *might* have been used on a battle fleet at sea or upon heavy troop concentrations or war material solely, cannot be overlooked. It is important, however, to recall the ways in which they have in fact been used, in considering their future uses.

This was undoubtedly in the minds of the members of the Permanent Commission of the Assembly of the French hierarchy in their impressive statement of June 1950, signed by nine Cardinals and Archbishops.

> People today are asking insistently whether we condemn the use of this atomic weapon. Such a question, addressed to the disciples of Christ, shocks and horrifies them. No one who has a "true sense of humanity", as His Holiness Pope Pius XII said two years ago, can fail to censure the use of all those modern weapons which strike indiscriminately at combatants and

that the city was crowded with refugees at the time of the attack was coincidental and took the form of a bonus". According to Swiss observers the total of dead was in the region of 100,000. In a petroleum bomb raid on Tokyo in 1945, prior to the atomic explosions, neutral observers estimated that 180,000 lost their lives in a single night.

Of the raids on Hiroshima and Nagasaki, the late U.S. Secretary of War, Harry Stimson, wrote in *On Active Service in Peace and War*, "The decision to use the atomic bomb was a decision which brought death to over a hundred thousand Japanese. No explanation can change that fact, and I do not wish to gloss it over. But this deliberate, premeditated destruction was our least abhorrent choice".

civilian populations and which scatter death blindly over areas more widespread in proportion as the scientific power of man increases. For our part, we condemn them with all our strength, as we did not hesitate to condemn during the last war the mass bombardments which, in attacking military objectives struck down at the same time old men, women and children. We are convinced that humanity dishonours the intelligence which God has given it, if it turns to evil a science which could be so fruitful for good.

On 19 October 1953, Pope Pius XII told an International Congress of Military Physicians:

It is not sufficient to have to defend oneself against any injustice in order to have recourse to the violent method of war. When the harm done by this cannot compare with that of "tolerated injustice", one may have the obligation to "suffer the injustice". All this is particularly true of "A.B.C. war". As for the question whether such warfare can become simply necessary in self-defence against "A.B.C. war", let it suffice that we have asked the question. The answer may be reached from principles that apply to war in general. In any case, another question has to be asked: Is it not possible to proscribe and successfully avoid "A.B.C. war" by international understanding?[1]

In his Easter Message, 1954, the Pope added:

For our part, we will tirelessly endeavour to bring about, by means of international agreements—always in subordination to the principle of legitimate self-defence . . . —the effective proscription and banishment of atomic, biological and chemical warfare.[2]

With the hydrogen bomb the possibilities of destruction increase still further. They increase to a point where the discus-

[1] AAS xxxv-II-xx, p. 730 ss.
[2] AAS xxxvi-II-xxi, p. 212 ss.

sion of military and non-military targets, the proportion of damage caused to non-combatants *per accidens*, and the question of discrimination at all, becomes utterly unreal. It is difficult, in the first place, to conceive of any military objective that an opposing enemy would present which would require even a "Hiroshima-type" atomic bomb to effect its destruction. But what kind of "legitimate" target is envisaged for the reception of an H-bomb?[1] The answer to this question can be obtained to some extent through the study of official Government documents and the statements of responsible political and military leaders. (The question is, of course, crucial at many points in this book.)

If the megaton-range H-bomb is not designed for discriminate use (except perhaps in discriminating between Manchester and Bradford), it cannot be properly controlled within the limits of moral and international law.

In his address to the World Medical Association of 30 September 1954, the Pope categorically declared:

Should the evil consequences of adopting this method of warfare ever become so extensive as to pass utterly beyond the control

[1] In contrast to the view expressed by the French hierarchy in 1950, on the question of nuclear weapons, the following extract from a sermon preached by Dr. Godfrey, Archbishop of Westminster, on Easter Day, 1958, is important: "Granted that a war of self-defence can be just, the State is in duty bound to do all possible to defend its essential life adequately. We do not believe that it has yet been conclusively shown that there can be no conceivable circumstances in which there might be a legitimate target for even the most powerful nuclear weapon. If this be so, then a nation would be justified in testing such weapons, unless again it be proved that the evil resulting therefrom outweighs the usefulness of the test". He goes on, however, "Nobody can subscribe to the thesis that it would ever be morally lawful to use indiscriminate nuclear weapons on centres of population which are predominantly civilian".

of man, then indeed its use must be rejected as immoral. In that event, it would no longer be a question of "defence" against injustice and necessary "protection" of legitimate possessions, but of the annihilation, pure and simple, of all human life within the affected area. That is not lawful on any title.[1]

The grave effects of radiation, genetically, and to fruitful soil, could be on a vast and uncontrollable scale in any major nuclear war. Pope Pius XII refers to this in his Easter Message of 1954:

They [atomic, biological and chemical weapons] are capable of causing the total extermination of all plant and animal life and of all works of man over ever wider regions. These weapons now make possible a sustained contamination of the atmosphere, the earth and the oceans with artificially produced radio-active isotopes of extended half-life; this even in areas far from the zones directly stricken and contaminated by the nuclear explosions. . . .
In this connection we do not wish to omit a reference to the danger for future generations from genetic mutations, attainable or perhaps already attained by new means of deviating the patrimony of man's hereditary factors from their natural development.[2]

4. TOWARDS A UNITED WITNESS?

In principle, so long as no international juridical authority exists with the necessary power to enforce its decisions, the right of a nation to defend itself against actual attack, remains the same, as it always has been.

This is made plain in the following passage from Pope Pius

[1] AAS xxxxvi-II-xxi, p. 587 ss. (This address refers to biological and chemical, as well as atomic warfare.)
[2] AAS xxxxvi-II-xxi, p. 212 ss.

XII's Christmas Message of 1956 (the year of the Hungarian rising):

> It is clear that in the present circumstances there can be verified in a nation the situation wherein every effort to avoid war being expended in vain, war—for effective self-defence and with the hope of a favourable outcome against unjust attack—could not be considered unlawful.
>
> If, therefore, a body representative of the people and a government—both having been chosen by free elections—in a moment of extreme danger decide, by legitimate instruments of internal and external policy, on defensive precautions, and carry out the plans which they consider necessary, they do not act immorally; so that a Catholic citizen cannot invoke his own conscience in order to refuse to serve and fulfil those duties the law imposes.[1]

But just as the right of self-defence remains intact, so the traditional qualifications of this right continue to limit its scope.[2]

All the conditions required for a just war, are mentioned in the above statement: lawful authority—"a body repre-

---

[1] AAS xxxxix-II-xxiv, p. 5 ss.

[2] Nowhere, perhaps, has the Christian idea of force being subject to law been elucidated more clearly than in Pope Pius XI's Encyclical letter to the Mexican Hierarchy, *Firmissimam Constantiam*, Easter Sunday 1937. Although concerned there with resistance to an unjust government, these general principles apply also to a war of defence.
1. That the methods used for indicating these rights are means to an end, or constitute a relative end, not a final and absolute end.
2. That, as means to an end, they must be lawful and not intrinsically evil acts.
3. That since they should be means proportionate to the end, they must be used only in so far as they serve to attain that end, in whole or in part, and in such a way that they do not bring greater harm to the community than the harm they were intended to remedy.

sentative of the people and a government—both having been chosen by free elections"; just cause—"war—for effective defence"; right intention—"decide, by legitimate instruments of internal and external policy, on defensive precautions"; last resort—"every effort to avoid war being expended in vain" and "in a moment of extreme danger"; moral certainty of success—"with the hope of a favourable outcome against unjust attack".[1]

Papal addresses and encyclicals are, on the whole, concerned with general principle. They are often made on occasions when Christian leaders, groups and individuals need to be reminded of the tenets they share, in order that they may, in their several capacities, relate them to the particular facts of the situation. In so many cases full knowledge of these facts is not immediately available to the central teaching authority, and even when it is, prudence and avoidance of political involvement may prohibit comment or action. Diversity of emphasis in different statements may thus tend to mislead those who have kept themselves insufficiently informed. Similarly, a reliance on direct affirmations alone is likely to result in a lack (if not deliberate avoidance) of further thought and deduction on the part of Catholics. This responsibility, however, cannot be avoided. A passage already quoted, from the Papal address to the Military Physicians Congress, 1953, is an explicit reminder of this:

[1] There are few moralists who would attempt to justify a "preventive" war. Pope Pius XII refers to "a moment of extreme danger" and Cardinal Ottaviani to "actual attack". Mgr. Ancel, Auxiliary Bishop of Lyons, in December 1951, warned French Catholics in the Lyons weekly, *Essor*: "Promoters of preventive war are war criminals, and any Catholic who really wishes the Americans to engage in a preventive war against Russia flagrantly violates the Sixth Commandment".

As for the question whether such warfare can become simply necessary in self-defence against "A.B.C. war", let it suffice that we have asked the question. The answer may be reached from principles that apply to war in general.

A reluctance to seek the answers, and to wait exclusively upon authority, must have bad effects on the Church as a whole. To avoid misunderstanding here, a paragraph from an essay by the eminent Jesuit theologian, Karl Rahner, will help to put the point more plainly:

> Do we not at present witness a neglect by the good and religious Christian of his duty to decide, imposed on him as an individual? Is there not a glancing toward the Church for instructions which either are in fact unfortunately not given, or else cannot be given at all, and hence are not to be expected? Is there not a cowardly inactivity because no instructions from above are at hand?[1]

In some matters, Pope Pius XII has been more explicit. He has stressed the necessity and obligation to outlaw aggressive war and more particularly to proscribe and banish atomic, biological and chemical warfare. The renunciation of nuclear weapon tests is spoken of as "an obligation in conscience, of nations and of their leaders". The need to support supranational authorities, such as U.N.O., in the work of justice and peace, has been stressed on more than one occasion.

The present Pope, in his first broadcast address of October 1958, *Urbi et Orbi*, made the following appeal to the rulers of all nations:

> Turn your eyes to the people entrusted to your care, and listen to them. What do they ask, what do they implore of you? They do not ask for those monstrous war machines produced in our

[1] "The Individual in the Church", *Stimmen der Zeit*, 1946, pp. 261 ff.

time which threaten to bring fratricidal massacres and world-wide havoc, but peace; that peace which would enable the human family freely to live, flourish and thrive.

Pope John's encyclical letter, *Ad Petri Cathedrum*, of June 1959, takes up the same theme:

> If we declare ourselves brothers and are brothers, and if we are called to the same destiny in this present life, and in the life to come, how can we possibly treat one another as adversaries and as enemies? How bear enmity to one another, cherish hatred and prepare deadly weapons against brothers? Already there has been enough fighting among men. Too many men in the flower of their life have shed their blood. Too many cemeteries of men slain in war cover the earth, and give us a solemn warning to lose no time before restoring concord, unity and a just peace.

Later in the same encyclical, Pope John speaks of the need to attain brotherly concord among nations and utters this grave warning:

> If the nations of the world do not achieve a fraternal union of this sort, which must be founded on justice and sustained by charity, the world situation will remain very serious. Thinking men very rightly deplore this state of suspense, which leaves in doubt whether we are travelling towards a real and solidly based peace or drifting in utter blindness towards a new and frightful war. In utter blindness, We say, for if indeed (which may God avert!) a new war should break out, the power of the monstrous new weapons is such that all the nations, victors and vanquished alike, would be left with nothing but a scene of universal ruin and destruction.

As little notice has been given by Catholics, by and large, to the Church's mission for international justice and peace, as to its teaching on social justice and the economic order. An

uncritical acceptance of a secularist society built upon in-
dustrial-capitalist foundations has led inevitably to an uncritical acceptance of that society's policies in the international field. Many of these policies, backed as they are by
the slogan "Peace through Strength", look to the threat of
force as their final arbiter. Coupled with this is a general indifference to the urgent needs of those countries and communities which are underclothed and underfed.

The prospect of communism has filled many Christians with
fear, a fear which paralyzes the reason and saps their moral
courage. A fear, moreover, which leads them to accept, sometimes unwittingly, motives of expediency to justify the most
questionable aspects of national defence policies. There seems
to be too great a readiness to permit political and military
leaders to make far-reaching decisions for themselves and
others in matters of grave moral consequence. The warning
of the late Archbishop McNicholas, O.P., of Cincinatti, in his
Lenten Pastoral of 1938, is urgently relevant today:

> Governments that have no fixed standards of morality and con-
> sequently no moral sense can scarcely settle the question of war
> on moral grounds for Christians.

The explosions at Hiroshima and Nagasaki did not give
rise to appropriate consternation and horror among Christians
in general. After so much violence, so much destruction,
people had become inured to the further final stages. The
possibility of its repetition on a far larger scale must remind
Catholics of a duty, uniquely urgent, to decide whether a
large-scale war, total and nuclear, can be reconcilable with
the principles of the Just War and whether the policy of deterrence (which rests on an ultimate willingness to commit oneself to such a war) is justifiable in the light of that teaching.

There will still be those, without doubt, who will wait for

the most authoritative statement from high ecclesiastical authority. Many will feel genuinely unable to come to a decision. One responsibility, and urgent duty, will remain theirs, however—to pray for guidance. May it come. And in good time.

VI

PRUDENCE, CONSCIENCE AND FAITH

Walter Stein

1. CALCULATING INCALCULABLES

If the argument of this book is valid, any large-scale use of nuclear weapons would be wicked. Further, any reliance on these weapons as "deterrents" must also be wicked, since this not only involves risks of their eventual use but hypothetically commits us to murder, here and now. And since, evidently, no major recourse to violence could henceforth be effective without nuclear weapons, it follows that violence, at any rate on a world-war scale, is now morally ruled out.

We have emphasized that our case does not rest on any sort of general objection to the employment of force by states. We deny the pacifist position, and maintain that states have the right, and the duty, to protect their communities against unjust attack, so long as they do so by means that themselves accord with justice. In the past, wars—even the most terrible wars—*could* be fought honourably and even nobly, although time and time again they in fact degenerated into murderous licence. It is only with the most recent technological advances that major war—and hence the threat of such a war—has become inherently atrocious.

That this is what has now happened seems so primitively evident that there may well seem to be something a little grotesque about an elaborate enquiry such as this, to establish that it has indeed happened. But the facts themselves are grotesque: above all, the fact that this unparalleled moral landslide seems to have taken place with so little apparent response. Unconditional pacifists continue, of course, to denounce the evils of war—and non-pacifists (with the usual professions of respect) continue to discount them. Politicians are content to rely on pre-nuclear modes of appeal, the press is content to echo the politicians, Christian opinion is divided and ineffective. No wonder, perhaps, that for instance in Britain, the Campaign for Nuclear Disarmament has itself so often relied on appeals to expediency. Apart from its traditional-pacifist wing, its exponents—whether theoretical thinkers like Lord Russell, strategists like Sir Stephen King-Hall, journalists like Philip Toynbee, or intellectuals of the "New Left"—all have sought to challenge the generals and politicians on their own ground, and to carry the public with them in terms of strategic and political considerations. In this process, the *moral* novelty of the situation is too easily taken for granted—or at any rate, there seems to be the assumption that morality is not enough, that the morally right course must be shown to coincide (very fortunately) with a balance of foreseeable advantages—or morality is in fact altogether discounted, the better to establish the "realism" of this sort of thinking.

It is easy to see why objectors to nuclear armaments should place so much stress on the expediency of their submissions. We have already (in Chapter I) touched on arguments of this kind and certainly do not wish to belittle the importance of this line of thought. Only by pressing these questions to the limit can we responsibly confront our situation. The danger is that, in our anxiety to achieve a maximum persuasiveness (towards ourselves as well as towards others) we might be led to push this kind of thinking far beyond its appropriate boundaries.

Unfortunately, this is just what has tended to happen in

discussions of nuclear policy. The more stubbornly the ad
cates of established policies have insisted on our strategic a
political dependence on "the deterrent", the more unco
promisingly have their opponents proclaimed its comple
strategic and political uselessness. Where the one side ca
see no security or hope but in our nuclear strength—if only
as a counter in disarmament negotiations—the other de-
nounces the possession of nuclear weapons as in fact the
greatest of our perils—in Britain's case, uselessly attracting a
preventive strike in case of war. In the one view, a world en-
slaved and corrupted by communism is the primary fear; in
the other, a world either annihilated, or reduced to chaos
and savagery. No wonder if, on each side, the temptation to
ignore, or undervalue, the other's emphasis has too often prevailed: in the face of *these* alternatives, our habitual calculations break down before the facts.

The trouble is that, again and again, we all the same insist
on returning to these calculations. And if no balance of decisive advantages exists, we find it necessary to invent one.
On both sides there seems to be the assumption that, whilst
wickedness may be wickedness, this of course is not sufficient
to disturb anything or anyone in the actual world. And so
both continue to accumulate proofs (and there are disturb-
ingly powerful proofs on both sides) that the other course
is impossible; that, whatever the risks of the policy advocated,
the opposite risks are worse.

Thus, whilst unilateral disarmers tend to denounce established policies as "madness", apologists for these policies re-
spond by diagnosing unilateralism as a failure of nerve as well
as brains: a reference to "practical politics" will then intro-
duce some well-matured sentences on the need for "calm and
careful judgment", on "security" and "the balance of power",
on the pursuit of "peace through strength", on "diplomatic

skill" and "patient negotiation", on "necessary guarantees and safeguards", on "adequate *quid pro quo's*". Some of these phrases, however threadbare, point to something that must still be taken seriously, but it is hardly surprising if many of those preoccupied with the nature of the "strength" that has now entered the world should feel them to be unspeakably irrelevant to present facts. They do not, even in the most rudimentary way, appear to reflect the condition of which Professor P. M. S. Blackett has said that some five or ten hydrogen bombs would suffice to knock Britain out of a war, "however well prepared with passive and civil defence organization, and however high the morale",[1] or concerning which General Gavin, as Chief of the United States Army Research and Development, testified to a Senate Committee, as early as 1956, that an "assault in force" against Russia was estimated to "run on the order of several hundred million deaths; that would be either way, depending upon which way the wind blew. If the wind blew to the south-east, they would be mostly in the U.S.S.R., although they would extend into the Japanese, and perhaps into the Philippine area. If the wind blew the other way, they would extend well back into Western Europe".[2] Meanwhile, an authoritative American study has estimated that an attack directed against the people of the U.S.A., totalling 2,000 megatons, would—through fall-out alone—kill 55 per cent of the population; 5,000 megatons would kill 80 per cent; and 20,000 megatons perhaps 100 per cent. (If the attack were directed only at military bases, 50,000 megatons would also destroy the entire population.)[3]

[1] "Atomic Weapons and East-West Relations", quoted by Philip Noel-Baker, *The Arms Race*, p. 170.

[2] *The Arms Race*, p. 170.

[3] "The Distribution and Effects of Fall-out in Large Nuclear Weapons Campaigns", by Everett and Pugh, of the Institute for Defence Analysis

It is easy to see how those who have urgently faced the meaning of nuclear war might be led to a simple inversion of orthodox attitudes—and tactics of persuasion. The menace is so overwhelming, and their opponents seem so unmoved, that it is hard to be serious about opposite risks and to recognize the relevance of other claims. Thus, at the 1960 Labour Party Conference, Mr. Michael Foot re-emphasized the "enormous risk" attaching to Britain's N.A.T.O. bases, Mr. Cousins deplored the cost of "a useless defence", and Mr. Mikardo denied nuclear weapons any deterrent value at all— they only ensured that Britain would "act as a lightning conductor or decoy duck to draw enemy fire on our heads and divert it from New York and Chicago".[1]

But, whatever force there may be in such objections to the "deterrent" (neatly crystallized in the Vicky cartoon where a John Bull/Minister of Defence, faced by a Bear, resolutely points a gun at his own head: "One step, and I shoot"), they are one-sided and overstated: no amount of juggling with the paradox of reciprocal suicide can conjure away the "balance of terror" itself. This "balance" may, from time to time, undergo relative shifts, and it cannot indefinitely guarantee peace. Nevertheless, it continues to be a present—as it is already a historical—determinant in our situation, and neither Britain's direct contribution nor those of nations serving only as bases for American weapons are negligible in this context. It simply is not the case that the gun is pointing solely at our-

---

in Washington, *Journal of Operations Research*, 1959, Vol. 7. Quoted by M. C. Berenbaum, *New Statesman*, 3 September 1960. Dr. Berenbaum points out that the present American stockpile is estimated as equivalent to 28,000 megatons, the Russian stockpile being probably nearly of the same order.

[1] *The Labour Party Conference 1960, The Guardian Report.*

selves—and what serves very well for a cartoon will not do as a serious judgment of our condition.

Any undervaluing—within its limits—of "the deterrent" is all the more objectionable if there is also insufficient aliveness to the risks of a possible communist domination. There are some who would not be disturbed by such an outcome: they are entitled to their beliefs, but those who disagree with them have cause to treat their concern for Western disarmament with some reserve. There are others who consider military aggression unlikely: but they really should remember Hungary and Tibet; and ought to bear in mind that there are other means besides overt warfare in which military power can be employed—from the Czech *coup d'état* under Stalin to Mr. Khrushchev's fierce menaces in times of crisis. And there are some who simply affirm the sufficiency of conventional weapons: it is time they came to grips with *Defence in the Nuclear Age*. It may be necessary to dispense with our "deterrent". But we should not demand its sacrifice on false pretences.

Clearly it is as hard for unilateralists to accept the full burden of their position as it is for others to accept as *now real* the real possibility of nuclear war. Even Stephen King-Hall and Bertrand Russell have to some extent played down their burdens. Thus Commander King-Hall—who was one of the first to recognize the implications of nuclear weapons, and whose voice remains one of the most trustworthy in these discussions—has stripped off many illusions, this side of "the thought-barrier in defence thinking". He was quick to expose the absurdities of "nuclear defence", to draw attention to the limitations of "nuclear deterrence"—and above all, to accept the logic of "escalation": since physical violence, in any major conflict, is now ultimately subject to the violence of nuclear weapons, the rejection of nuclear weapons must, in reason, involve the rejection of all other physical means of defence in such a conflict. Only a strategy of non-violence remains open on these assumptions; and Sir Stephen's *Defence in the Nuclear Age* proceeds to outline one. At this point, however, a questionable optimism takes charge of his case.

This was brought out very sharply when, soon after the publication of his book, its findings were challenged by Professor David Mitrany, in an impressive letter to *The Guardian*. I should like to cite from this letter at some length:

Non-resistance [i.e. Sir Stephen's "non-violent resistance"] demands a very high degree of self-restraint and self-sacrifice, of which in any country only very few are likely to prove capable. With others it may be weakness or fear, or the sheer human need to keep oneself and one's family alive. But apart from that there have always been large numbers who, whether sincere sympathizers or merely callous opportunists, are likely to split the outlook of the resisting group.

In the case of a communist occupier the numbers willing to collaborate are likely to be much larger than in the case of the Nazis. And that is really the main aspect that Sir Stephen overlooks. Having set out to destroy a purely military point of view, he in fact looks at the problem likewise only from a military standpoint. But an occupation by the Russians would not be an ordinary military occupation; it would be a *revolutionary* occupation, with an ideological purpose and drive behind it. Apart from attracting very probably, therefore, the sympathy of many groups, it is also likely, as in civil wars, to be much more ruthless in its ways and ends. The Geneva Conventions have never played any part in civil wars. An attack or an occupation which is spurred by some fanatical ideal (whether of racial, or class, or religious "salvation") looks upon any resistance as a vicious reaction and treats it accordingly as something not to be merely defeated but uprooted. The consequence of this is that "democratic" non-resistance for the purpose of salving the democratic way of life is, sadly, a vain hope. . . . Obviously, when Sir Stephen contemplates the fine moral results that might come from non-resistance, even at the cost of some material discomfort or suffering, he thinks in terms of the way in which the Americans and ourselves would treat a non-resisting group. . . . He might have learnt something from what is happening in Algeria; and he certainly should have learnt something from the way the Soviet Communists, who are after all the chief factor concerned in this issue, have dealt with resisting, or indeed with merely suspected, groups in the countries they have occupied.

It might be easy for some of us to sacrifice ourselves; it would not be human to stand by and look on while one's family was starved or mutilated; and no political leader could call upon a whole people to accept such political immolation.

The conclusion is that non-resistance may save our skin, or some of it, but will not save our way of life—which is what Sir Stephen thinks of achieving. And in the meantime the emotional confusion fed by such appeals will deflect our minds and efforts from the only possible way to peace, by positive international action.[1]

Those whose most fundamental commitments are religious would need to complete Professor Mitrany's account by reference to the immensely efficient persecutions of the Church in China, Hungary and other satellite countries—not only the physical and psychological sufferings of its members, but the schismatic infiltrations, the unscrupulous propaganda, the insistent, insidious pressure towards apostasy, and the conditioning of youth with all the resources of official education. It is neither meanness nor fanaticism that leads one to kick against such a prospect. "Anything rather than this!"

[1] *The Guardian*, 21 March 1958.

And yet—anything? Even an H-bomb war? As Bertrand Russell has said, there may be some question whether half the population of the world would survive, or a quarter, or none. What is certain is that, at best, such a world "would consist of destitute populations, maddened by hunger, debilitated by disease, deprived of the support of modern industry and means of transport, incapable of supporting educational institutions, and rapidly sinking to the level of ignorant savages".[1] Leaving aside the tremendous question of genetic effects, really: *anything?* Neither free government nor the spiritual life is likely to flourish in such a world.

Yet again, if we should reel back towards unconditional disarmament, may we not be preparing the way for an equally incalculable outcome? Lord Russell underestimates both the immediate threat of communism and its more long-term dangers. "There have been bad Governments and bad systems in the past. Genghis Khan, for example, was quite as bad as fanatical anti-communists believe Stalin to have been. But his tyranny did not last for ever, and if his enemies had had the power to extinguish human life rather than submit to his brutalities, nobody in the present day would regret their not having exercised this power."[2] But Ghengis Khan had no Communist Party behind him, no Leninism, no modern thought-control techniques, no guns or aeroplanes—and, for that matter, no H-bombs. Is it, then, "unhistorical" (as Lord Russell suggests) to have misgivings even about the more distant future? Or is it not rather unhistorical to argue from analogy where all analogy has so plainly broken down (just as unhistorical as those who claim to be guided by historical experience in clinging to the H-bomb)? We simply cannot say what would happen. And though—when all has been said—

[1] *Common Sense and Nuclear Warfare*, p. 42.
[2] *Op. cit.*, p. 75.

Lord Russell and those who think along these lines have good grounds to persist even so in describing a communist domination as the "lesser evil", is language not cracking under the strain? Such a "lesser evil" might be more than we could bear.

And there there is one further, crucial consideration: it is *risks* rather than outcomes that have to be weighed. "A "worse risk" may be a risk of a worse thing or a more probable risk of a less bad thing. Those who defend the policy of "deterrence" freely admit that if the great war we fear breaks out, then the policy has failed and all is lost: they are just betting that our governments can edge along the tight-rope. They agree that what lies below is an abyss of destruction, but they think that we may not fall into it, whereas if the West gave up its present policy the "lesser evil" would become a certainty: to abandon the deterrent is thus felt to be the *graver risk*. Of course, in another sense the "graver risk" remains simply identical with the *greater evil*, but how are these two types of "gravity" to be related? What objective criteria could be appealed to, to arbitrate between them? Even if one is satisfied that, in the extremity of our dilemma, we can meaningfully go on speaking of a "greater" and a "lesser" evil at all, what, finally, is to decide the issue between such a "greater evil" and such a "graver risk"?

It is significant that, in his reply to Professor Mitrany, Sir Stephen King-Hall could only reply (i) that, if his plan were adopted, a military occupation by the Soviet Union would be a "most improbable" tactic, (ii) that "an *ad hoc* movement struggling to life after a military defeat is something qualitatively different" from what he is proposing, (iii) that "Professor Mitrany and all those who had seized on this one aspect of my defence plan seem to have no understanding of the monstrous dangers and deficiencies of our present arrangements".

The first two of these points are, at best, speculative. It is the third that really tells. But only by balancing Professor Mitrany's emphasis—just as Professor Mitrany only succeeds in balancing Sir Stephen's.

Sir Stephen's reply concludes:

> Having dismissed my comprehensive plan by dealing with one aspect of it, Professor Mitrany gives us his formula for peace in the three words: *positive international action*. What does this cliché add up to in March 1958? I call for positive *national* action.

And here indeed, is the rub. As times goes on, things look now more, now less promising for "positive international action"; but real international control can now only mean world-*government*. (Nothing short of this could enforce an agreement in future crises; nothing short of such powers of enforcement can provide the security Professor Mitrany is in search of.) If, however, we were even beginning to be ready for world-government, we should not so urgently need it. The need is immense; the obstacles firmly anchored in this need. It is one of the ironies of our present condition that the story of the earthquake pills—on sale at the time of the Lisbon earthquake (for "what else would you suggest"?)—is now as applicable to the toughest diplomatic "realists" as to the "Utopians" against whom it used to be told. With ideologies desperately confronting each other, bombs and missiles springing up right and left all over the globe, and a long queue of applicants for admission into The Club, what would you suggest in place of positive international action?

The fact is, neither international action, not the strategic *status quo*, nor unilateral disarmament can produce a condition of pre-nuclear comfort. None of these can dissolve the fact of the East-West struggle for existence. And no adding up of relative advantages can appear entirely convincing, or even entirely sane, so long as the other side of the balance-sheet is kept in view.

Our civilization is in many ways built upon the power to calculate. This power is, of course, splendid, it is one of the things in virtue of which we are human. But our humanity also places limits on calculation. These limits can easily be missed, and perhaps for too long now we have tended to miss them. Now there is fire on the horizon, like writing on a wall.

2. ABSOLUTE AND RELATIVE

There is no necessary gap between morality and prudence. Indeed, the majority of moral principles are simply codifications of prudence. The object of prudence is well-being, the individual's or the community's general interest. Sometimes there may be some tension between individual and communal —or between various communities'—general interest. It is then that we tend most readily to feel "under obligation": "conscience" now takes charge of our problem, and arbitrates amidst the conflicting claims. Usually, however, it still arbitrates in terms of prudential considerations. I must not only love my neighbour as myself, but must try to know what it is that love would prudently do in this or that situation. I must try to discover the nature of his real needs (that is, the deficiencies in his well-being) and so the appropriate means towards his completion. It would not only be unwise, it would also be immoral if a doctor took unnecessary risks with a habit-forming drug. Similarly, it would not only be inexpedient but *wrong* if a government failed to afford the greatest possible protection to its subjects, or if a general lost more lives than he must.

Common sense—and even most moralists—would probably more or less agree up to this point. But disagreements are certain to multiply as soon as it is claimed that there may, at times, be a clash between morality and empirical interest—and, in this sense, a clash between morality and prudence. The classical instance is that of the man confronted by X, angrily brandishing a gun, and asking whether Y is in the next room. Should the man tell a lie to save Y's life? Could it actually be *wrong*, here, to take the obvious precaution? One might say that all the most important ethical disputes, from Machiavelli and Hobbes, or Bentham and Kant, to Sartre and contemporary English moralists like R. M. Hare and P. H. Nowell-Smith, are implicit in these questions.

If this text-book problem should seem somewhat unreal (though one can easily envisage actual situations of this kind), one might refer to a long series of similar problems at the heart of recent ferments in our way of life. Does marriage continue to bind, even though this should involve a maximum of unhappiness all round? Is pre-marital intercourse not justified by releasing adolescent tensions and ensuring more mature selection in marriage? Can the use of contraceptives be immoral if it assists both the fulfilment of nuptial love and the family's well-being as a whole? Indeed, can it be other than *obligatory* in a world already heavily over-populated and continuing to increase at tremendous rates just where it is already most overcrowded? Or again: may abortion be justified in certain circumstances, especially if this alone offers hope of saving the mother's life? May euthanasia, in some circumstances, not be a duty? Must a state observe moral rules, even though it may thus injure its citizens? Must it *always*, for instance, observe treaty commitments, even though in some particular case doing so appears to threaten the peace? May it, in extreme need, have recourse to torture, as a means of securing vital information? Or inflict collective punishments, where individual rebels have eluded its search?

The questions could be considerably prolonged, though these are some of the most important. In confronting them, people will tend to fall into two clearly defined groups, all along the line, though with some of the examples they might wish, for various reasons, to cross over to the other side.

The problem behind all these problems is whether morality and prudence (in the sense in which I have used the term) must necessarily coincide. It is just because, in such cases, there are at least *prima facie* reasons for thinking that prudential humaneness may be in tension with general moral principles that our ebbing traditions have left a litter of clashing relativities behind them. On the one hand, there are the continued appeals to moral absolutes; on the other hand, a wide variety of approaches rejecting the unconditional authority of such norms. In the one case, as we have seen, the principle of double effect, bounding the areas of human responsibility, serves as the guardian of unconditional obligations; in the other, conceptions of responsibility so unlimited that everything we do or—however remotely—*permit* is conceived as equally "our doing": so that nothing, in the end, seems determinately ours at all—and "necessary evils" begin to proliferate all over the field of moral conduct.

Some objections to this concept of "necessary evils" have already been urged, in Chapter I. And most of this book has been devoted to an analysis of one absolutely intolerable course of action that we have collectively set out on—precisely as a "necessary evil". From one point of view, the debate of the last few years on nuclear policy is simply a continuation of the long debate, at every level of our civilization, between absolute and relative moralities—or (to put it another way) between prudence circumscribed and prudence absolute. What distinguishes the present debate from anything that has preceded it is the fact that unrestricted prudence can no longer find its way about, even on its own terms. It is as if Kafka's parable had been given an ultimate finality:

"Alas", said the mouse, "the world is growing smaller every day. At the beginning, it was so big that I was afraid, I kept running and running, and I was glad when at last I saw walls far away to the right and left, but those long walls narrowed so quickly that I am in the last chamber already, and here in the corner stands the trap that I must run into". "You only need to change your direction", said the cat, and ate it up.

Was it wholly sane after all to imagine that prudence—whether social or private—can settle every problem? As when statesmen and journalists and respected academics urbanely dismiss moral absolutes from this debate? Or when such a passionate objector to nuclear weapons as Mr. Philip Toynbee confessed in The Fearful Choice that he "would go on choosing lesser evils right up to the end"[1]—so that if it could be shown "that unless one tortured" (and killed) "a million children ten million would certainly be tortured (and killed) he would think it "right" to torture the million?[2]

On this plane, it is Mr. Kingsley Amis—who not only accepts the sovereignty of "lesser evils" but has recorded a prudent dislike of "an irrational capacity to become inflamed by interests and causes that are not one's own, that are outside oneself"[3]—who accordingly has the last word:

I feel I would sooner be occupied by the Russians than atomized. But if that occupation meant being shot, or seeing my family die of starvation instead of radiation, I begin to feel a little less certain about that preference. But until I can be shown that the

[1] The Fearful Choice: A Debate on Nuclear Policy, edited by Philip Toynbee, p. 103.
[2] Op. cit., p. 109.
[3] Socialism and the Intellectuals (Fabian Society), p. 6.

chance of a savage Russian occupation of the kind I have described is significantly less than the chance of being atomized,
I'm prepared to see us going on as we are, horrible as that is. The
risks of unilateral disarmament frighten me to roughly the same
degree (it's impossible to be precise) as those of continuing
inside the American bloc.[1]

Here at last—if prudence is all—the fearful choice is confronted without evasions of any kind. Mr. Amis successfully
sheds all "interests and causes that are not one's own, that are
outside oneself"—and denies himself all illusory comforts. No
wonder he is paralyzed.

Paralysis, in these circumstances, is a wholly appropriate
state. It alone fully registers that openness to the facts that
each prudent disputant is so anxious to claim as his own. And,
facing the facts, it may find a way through. "Where does one
go from a world of insanity?/Somewhere on the other side
of despair."

For the determined insobriety of these discussions may be
traced back to the assumption that men can calculate the
future to a far greater extent than they can. It is a fact absolutely essential to the working of both prudence and morality
that "no man knows what another day will bring"; this fact
is grossly underestimated by both sides of our dispute. George
Kennan has said that he knows of no difficulties that we are
in now that cannot be related to the policy of "unconditional
surrender" in the last war. At the time, objections to that
policy were purely "moral". But morality would have been
long-term prudence. Short-term "prudence" that conflicts
with morality is likely to be the most imprudent thing in the
world. People are blinded to this by having too much confidence that they can calculate the future. In this confidence,
they talk in madder and madder styles. In fact, the policy of

[1] *The Fearful Choice*, p. 52.

keeping nuclear weapons is a mixture of short-term "prudence" and dark passions.

Arthur Koestler once dramatized how prudence (or "expediency") is related to morals in the modern world. Reminding us how expediency has tended to get increasingly out of hand, till we are threatened with "a kind of radioactive decay of all values", he proceeds to describe "the express train of mankind's progress".

> On this train expediency is the engine, morality the brake. The action of the two is always antagonistic. We cannot make an abstract decision in favour of one or the other. But we can make a temporary adjustment according to the train's progress. Two hundred years ago, during the train's laborious ascent from the stagnant marshes of feudal France towards the era of the Rights of Man, the decision would have been in favour of the engine and against the brake. Since about the second half of the nineteenth century our ethical brakes have been more and more neglected until the totalitarian dynamism made the engine run amok. We must apply the brake or we shall crash.[1]

One may have reservations about this image (expediency and morality are by no means "always atagonistic") but its very crudities are symptoms of the condition it describes. For it is precisely because Koestler has so urgently lived through tensions of this kind that his emergent absolutism is so impressive. His essay concludes:

> I am not so sure whether what the philosophers call ethical absolutes exist, but I am sure that we have to act as if they existed. Ethics must be freed from its utilitarian chains; words and deeds must again be judged by their own merits and not as mere makeshifts to serve distant and nebulous aims. These worm-eaten ladders lead to no paradise.

[1] "What the Modern World is Doing to the Soul of Man", in *The Challenge of Our Time* (Percival Marshall, 1948), p. 19.

The debate on nuclear weapons we have reviewed does not concern itself with paradises, its aims are confined to the most modest requirements for decent survival, yet these basic human aims have come to appear as elusive and retreating as the objects of the most rampant Utopianism. For our train is now careering into wild and unknown landscapes, with its engine completely out of control. Perhaps we shall yet apply the brakes, to be jerked out of our calculated insanities.

3. THE GATES OF HELL

The immediate demand upon us is quite simple and final: *Thou shalt not murder*. But, whether we are Christians or unbelievers, this demand, here and now, seems a very hard saying indeed. Even if we are impelled to comply unconditionally with it, we continually relapse into trying to make conditions. It could hardly be otherwise. Its present implications are so total that only a correspondingly total readjustment could match it.

On the practical plane, it just is not enough to say: very well, let us try to ensure that nobody will ever have occasion —or the opportunity—to use nuclear weapons, let us move towards international control. By all means let us try: nothing less will in fact do than a radically new international order— a unified world authority. But how can we hope to create such an order—how is this most intimate, authoritative unity to emerge out of mutual anathema and terror?

We cannot begin to imagine it. Two things are, however, certain. That it is not enough to say, let us try: in this matter, we must succeed; and that success will be more a matter of *willing* the means, than of merely discovering what these means ought to be. I have argued that to will the means to peace in our situation is to be ready to bear very grave risks indeed (though we cannot, anyway, avoid very grave risks of one kind or another). In effect, we should have to be prepared for unilateral disarmament (or an equivalent unilateral risk-taking—whatever the diplomatic formalities) and so ultimately for non-violent resistance.

For not only is a hard-boiled, genuinely *secure* disarmament agreement so remote in terms of the facts as to be hardly more than a block to fresher thinking; once we have recognized that nuclear war is not merely a catastrophic menace, but a *wickedness,*

That tears shall drown the wind

—we shall no longer want to await such a sound bargain before we abjure it.

Even if we should want to (in tribute, perhaps, to our unflappable practical sense), we shall have to recognize that, morally, we are involved in wickedness as soon as, and so long as, we are, in the last resort, committed to sanction such deeds—and that support for "the deterrent" commits one in this way.

We have striven, in this book, to defend these propositions with as much rigour as we could achieve. We have tried to preserve an appropriate detachment where this seemed to be called for, and to confess our passionate involvement where we felt we ought to confess it.

In the end, it is not, however, by arguments or counter-arguments that this question will be decided—not, of course, because it has nothing to do with reason, but because reason cannot but be radically tempted to have nothing to do with it. With so much, so desperately, at stake, and not merely a "thought-barrier" to be broken through, but barriers of the spirit even more challenging, what meaning can we give to "the other side of despair"?

For the writers of this book, the answer is, of course, a religious one. For Our Lord charges us: "Woe to the world

143

because of scandals. For it must needs be that scandals come: but nevertheless woe to the man by whom the scandal cometh. And if thy hand or foot scandalize thee, cut it off and cast it from thee. It is better for thee to go into life maimed or lame, than having two hands or two feet, to be cast into everlasting fire". But it is this same Lord of whom we say: "I know that my Redeemer liveth". Much is asked, but: "Peace I leave with you, my peace I give unto you: not as the world giveth, do I give unto you. Let not your heart be troubled, nor let it be afraid." Our cares are great and grave, but they are circumscribed. "Sufficient unto the day is the evil thereof". We cannot but say "yes" to unconditional demands. Even our care for the Church herself is ultimately set a term to: it would not *be* the Church but for the promise accompanying its mission: "and behold I am with you always, even to the consummation of the world".

Where these things are believed, there should be no panic —and no perplexity. As regards the immediate decisions to be taken, the paralyzing calculus of lesser evils is displaced by a simple, challenging absolute. (This is not, of course, the end of decisions to be taken but the beginning—a precondition to any realistic response to what confronts us). As regards the outcome of it all:

> Teach us to care and not to care
> Teach us to sit still.

We only know with certainty that no other response will do, and that the Gates of Hell will not prevail.

Can one, today, retain any sort of rational hope outside this Ark? Lord Russell, in his *Common Sense and Nuclear Warfare,* hopes "that some gleam of sanity may yet shine in the minds of statesmen. But the spread of power without wisdom is utterly terrifying, and I cannot much blame those whom it reduces to despair".[1] There is a note in this book whose latent reverberations could be far more profound than any of his actual proposals. He considers the possibility that, soon, we shall for instance have the means to control climates and geography in such ways as to be able to flood, or starve out, an enemy. Whilst such measures, he says, are not yet within reach, there are others which "have lately entered the domain of feasible lunacy". Satellites should soon be able to "rain death upon enemy regions, while suspending this useful activity during their passage over friendly territory". And then there is the business of space travel. This might seem a feat of disinterested scientific adventure. "But I am afraid that it is from baser motives that Governments are willing to spend the enormous sums involved in making space-travel possible".

General Putt, in evidence before the House Committee on Armed Services, explained that the United States Air Force aims at establishing a missile base on the moon to the earth without an enormous expenditure of energy, since the moon has no atmosphere and little gravity. He declared that the moon "might provide a retaliation base of considerable advantage over earth-bound nations". He pointed out that an attack upon the moon by the U.S.S.R. would have to be launched a day or two before an attack upon the terrestrial United States if the United States was to be unable to retaliate from the moon. Such a preliminary attack upon the moon, he considered, would warn Americans of their danger. If, on the other hand, the Russians did not demolish the United States lunar installations, it would be possible, from these installations, to destroy Russia although the terrestrial United States had been obliterated.

When, Lord Russell, continues, it was pointed out that, in that case, Russia must be expected to pursue a similar course "the moral which he drew was that the United States must also occupy Mars and Venus which, apparently, he considered to be beyond the reach of the Soviets". Lord Russell concludes:

> In reading of the plans of militarists, I try very hard to divest myself for the time being of the emotions of horror and disgust. But when I read of plans to defile the heavens by the petty squabbles of the animated lumps that disgrace a certain planet, I cannot but feel that the men who make these plans are guilty of a kind of impiety. It is easy to imagine a Congressional election, or a Soviety party dispute, turning on the question whether Americans on the moon have exterminated the Russians there or vice versa. Such plans degrade the heavenly bodies and the majestic course of nature to the petty stature of furious men quarrelling over trifles.[1]

"Trifles" or not, this surely is the only authentic human response to what we are being involved in; and does not a whole modern tradition reach out towards new awarenesses in this great sceptic's protest?—a cry as far removed from *The Conquest of Happiness* as Albany's avowal:

> If that the heavens do not their visible spirits
> Send quickly down to tame these vile offences,
> It will come,
> Humanity must perforce prey on itself,
> Like monsters of the deep

—is from Mephistopheles' reassurances to Faustus:

> Why Faustus,
> Thinkest thou heaven is such a glorious thing?
> I tell thee, 'tis not half so fair as thou,
> Or any man that breathes on earth. . . .

Could it be that these grotesque "impieties" against man and

---

[1] *Common Sense and Nuclear Warfare*, pp. 19-20.

nature might be re-awakening a sense of that inviolable—but violated—*ought*, whose very absoluteness could point to (and indeed could help to make present) "somewhere on the other side of despair"?

It would ill become those of us who are Christians to pursue these possibilities further, in theoretical terms. There is much to be done to assist the process just hinted at. But only through what we ourselves *do*: not by arguing a brief, but by bearing witness.

We are in any case forced to bear witness, here: first, simply to our humanity and obligations as men. There is no escape from this challenge. One rejects, or one accepts. One protests, or one condones.

Exactly the same holds on the other two levels at which our witness is required. Only, there is even more at stake. As individual Christians, what we thus do, or fail to do, cannot but be also an affirmation or denial of Our Lord. And by our individual behaviour (no man can say this without awe) others will be helped or hindered in their own moral and spiritual endeavours. They will tend to judge the nature, the fruits and the reality of our Faith by our faith.

In the end, however, our individual Christian witness is essentially a part of the collective witness of the Church. (I speak, of course, as a Roman Catholic). Whatever we do, or fail to do, is part of the Church's being. Pope, bishops, priests and laymen, *together are* the Church—through whom Christ is mediated to the world. Christ is present within the Church, especially within the Sacraments, irrespective of what any of us may do. But what we do, and what we are, cannot but make the Church's presence harder or easier to *see*. At all times, therefore, we are bearing witness—well or not so well, helping or hindering the manifestation of Christ-within-the-Church.

Today, the world's uniquely urgent problems of war and peace call upon the Church's witness with corresponding urgency. The Church, in its very nature, has a special mission for peace: because, as a human society it commands vast loyalties throughout the world, and because it is divine, headed by Christ himself. Its tradition on questions of war and peace reaches back to the Gospels themselves and only requires application to new circumstances and problems.

In principle, there is no reason why individual Catholics should not arrive at these applications for themselves (as we have sought to do in this book); indeed, they have a duty to do so, so far as they are able. Unfortunately, as experience has shown, there is in fact nearly as much confusion among the faithful, in this field, as there is outside the Church. This is perhaps understandable, in view of the immensely radical character of these problems and the enormous risks and sacrifices that are in question. Some of these confusions have been touched on at various points of this book.

But not even the long series of Papal and episcopal statements that have been traced in the previous chapter have sufficed to reduce these confusions to order. Many of these statements are extraordinarily impressive—and one might perhaps have expected that such formulations as Pope Pius XII's to the World Medical Association, of September 1954, and the French hierarchy's statement of 1950, would be hard to reconcile with subsequent apologies—or silences—on nuclear weapons. But no adequate Catholic witness has emerged.

Perhaps only the most solemn, authoritative pronouncement will suffice to bring this about. And whilst individual members of the Church may, and should, bear witness individually and in groups, may we not hope and pray for such a pronouncement?

As we have seen, whatever defects there may be in merely prudential arguments for unilateral disarmament—even on this plane alone, the policy of "deterrence" can be proved absurd. Sometimes the exponents of this line of thought have allowed themselves to overplay their hand, as for instance when they claim that the deterrent cannot even (within limits) be said to *deter*. More often, and more seriously, they have underestimated the alternative dangers that obsess apologists for nuclear weapons. And they rarely appreciate, with sufficient urgency, the sense in which unilateral disarmament can be held to involve the "graver"—because *more probable*—risk, even if nuclear war is agreed to be the "worse" —because even *more terrible*—risk if it should ever actually come to such a war. Nevertheless, their case is unanswerable in so far as it sets out to show: (i) that nuclear "deterrence" is *at best* a highly imperfect instrument of protection; (ii) that no military means at all can win for us the underlying "battle for minds"; (iii) that the implications of nuclear war are such that it could not, sanely, be chosen even in preference to the most appalling alternative; (iv) and that the uneasy "balance of terror" between such opponents can hardly fail to explode, sooner or later, into total nuclear war—even if neither side deliberately "chooses" to trigger it off.

This case suffices to prove the absurdity of "nuclear deterrence". Prudence itself cannot tolerate a posture so inadequate even in purely military terms, so impotent on the ideological plane, and so recklessly intemperate in its accepted risks. Prudence itself once and for all disowns the sanity of such a "defence". And yet—as we also saw—the predicament is so extraordinary that there remains this counter-claim on behalf of present policies: that unilateral disarmament also is absurd. If it is reckless to accept the risks of a nuclear war, it is reckless to place the whole world at the mercy of communism. (i)

Nuclear deterrence may not give us full security, but it does give protection within limits, and it is all the protection we have; (ii) only by employing it can we hope to gain time, to win the "battle for minds"; (iii) even if a communist triumph were agreed to be the "lesser evil", as compared with a nuclear war, it is nevertheless *so* appalling as to render its deliberate acceptance absurd; (iv) and, whilst the prevailing "balance of terror" *might*, with luck and good management, be prolonged without an explosion, unilateral disarmament could hardly fail to result in a communist domination.

Each case establishes the absurdity of the other; so that neither can establish the expediency of its own. Where everything is reduced to absurdity, some absurdities may be more absurd than others, but degrees of absurdity can hardly form a basis for rational choice. The two sets of arguments do not exactly cancel out, but the main effect of confronting them with each other is to paralyze their respective force. Once this nightmarish stalemate of inexpediencies is faced, expediency may be ready to abandon its sovereign pretensions, and—acknowledging its natural human limits—return to its own subordination to moral *law*.

But is it not merely that absolute morality thus lays claim to the renewed allegiance of those who had long supposed it dead; its immediate challenge is such that only faith—absolute, beyond all human calculations, a faith that can move fear—can summon the resources to meet its demands. By its unconditional preclusion of total war—and, equally, the hypothetical readiness to engage in such a war—morality transcends the apparent stalemate of "necessary evils" and redeems the alternative course from absurdity. But it is *only* in the light of faith that this alternative course can itself give ground for rational hope.

At bottom, therefore, the challenge transcends not only

prudence, but morality as well: to Christians it is a challenge to their faith; to unbelievers, to their unbelief. For, just as this radical, total challenge pushes Morals Without Religion (a perfectly legitimate commitment within its limits) to a point where it must either delude itself, or despair, or itself be totally transcended by faith, so faith is compelled to take stock of its own reality, asking itself whether it dares pronounce the promise that the Gates of Hell shall not prevail, whilst preparing to massacre the innocent in defence of the things of God. It is just because this converging double challenge, to Christians and non-Christians alike, is so ultimate and inescapable that it contains within its desperate appeal the hope of things that could, literally, be wonderful.

Unconditional disarmament would only be the first step. Measures like those outlined by Sir Stephen King-Hall would acquire an essential added dimension by a revival of Western religious energies. So would adequate aid to the hungry countries of the world. Without this religious dimension, non-violent resistance seems doomed. But the more the Church stands to lose, humanly speaking, by committing herself, and her mission, to these dangers, the more clearly her existence will be seen as a divine fact. The future may then safely be left to God. Pharaoh's armies may be close upon us and the Sea extend before our feet, but we know that our Redeemer liveth.